STUDENTS
AT THE
CENTER

ASCD MEMBER BOOK

Many ASCD members received this book as a
member benefit upon its initial release.

Learn more at: **www.ascd.org/memberbooks**

BENA
KALLICK

ALLISON
ZMUDA

STUDENTS
AT THE
CENTER

*Personalized Learning
with Habits of Mind*

Foreword by Arthur L. Costa

Alexandria, Virginia USA

1703 N. Beauregard St. • Alexandria, VA 223111714 USA
Phone: 800-933-2723 or 703-578-9600 • Fax: 703-575-5400
Website: www.ascd.org • E-mail: member@ascd.org
Author guidelines: www.ascd.org/write

Deborah S. Delisle, *Executive Director;* Robert D. Clouse, *Managing Director, Digital Content & Publications;* Stefani Roth, *Publisher;* Genny Ostertag, *Director, Content Acquisitions;* Julie Houtz, *Director, Book Editing & Production;* Katie Martin, *Editor*; Melissa Johnston, *Graphic Designer;* Mike Kalyan, *Director, Production Services;* Keith Demmons, *Senior Production Designer*

PAPERBACK ISBN: 978-1-4166-2324-3   ASCD product #117015
PDF E-BOOK ISBN: 978-1-4166-2326-7; see Books in Print for other formats.
Quantity discounts: 10–49, 10%; 50+, 15%; 1,000+, special discounts (e-mail programteam@ascd.org or call 800-933-2723, ext. 5773, or 703-575-5773). For desk copies, go to www.ascd.org/deskcopy.

ASCD Member Book No. FY17-4A (Jan. 2017 PSI+). Member books mail to Premium (P), Select (S), and Institutional Plus (I+) members on this schedule: Jan, PSI+; Feb, P; Apr, PSI+; May, P; Jul, PSI+; Aug, P; Sep, PSI+; Nov, PSI+; Dec, P. For details, see www.ascd.org/membership and www.ascd.org/memberbooks.

Library of Congress Cataloging-in-Publication Data

Names: Kallick, Bena, author.
Title: Students at the center : personalized learning with habits of mind / Bena Kallick and Allison Zmuda.
Description: Alexandria, Virginia : ASCD, 2017. | Includes bibliographical references and index.
Identifiers: LCCN 2016042387 | ISBN 9781416623243 (pbk.)
Subjects: LCSH: Individualized instruction. | Thought and thinking--Study and teaching.
Classification: LCC LB1031 .K345 2017 | DDC 371.39/4--dc23 LC record available at https://lccn.loc.gov/2016042387

26 25 24 23 22 21 20 19 18   3 4 5 6 7 8 9 10 11 12

For Grant Wiggins

This work rests on the shoulders of your teachings and
how you engaged with us and so many others. Your vitality,
intelligence, and joy continue to live in our work every day.

———————

To laugh often and much;
To win the respect of intelligent people
and the affection of children;
To earn the appreciation of honest critics
and endure the betrayal of false friends;
To appreciate beauty;
To find the best in others;
To leave the world a bit better,
whether by a healthy child, a garden
patch, or a redeemed social condition;
To know even one life has breathed
easier because you have lived;
This is to have succeeded.

—*Ralph Waldo Emerson*

———————

STUDENTS
AT THE
CENTER

Personalized Learning with Habits of Mind

Foreword

There is no learning that is not personalized. Anything "learned" must first be taken in through the senses, processed and understood, interiorized in the mind and body, and emotionally charged and acted upon. In this book, Bena Kallick and Allison Zmuda brilliantly describe personalized learning in terms of four powerful defining attributes—*voice, co-creation, social construction,* and *self-discovery*—and propose using them as filters to examine and enhance practice in classrooms designed for personalized learning.

This view of personalized learning is more than just a helpful framework for educators; it's also a way of thinking about an innate human quest that each of us is born into and pursues throughout our lifetime (Fogarty, 2016). Consider that the first action of newborn babies is to use their *voice* to announce themselves, crying to the world, "I'm here! I have arrived. Hear me, feed me, see me, cuddle me, change me, love me!" As children grow, their natural curiosity drives them to seek others who can help satisfy their urge to learn: "Teach me, show me, read to me, sing to me, answer my insatiable questions. And I want to do it myself!" Together—with parents or caregivers, teachers, and peers—children *co-create* an image of themselves, of the world and how it works, and of what it means to learn. Because human beings are social beings, young children soon discover the

x | *Students at the Center*

process of *social construction*, the bonding with others that unleashes the power of camaraderie, cooperative learning, and interdependent thinking. Thus starts a lifelong journey of *self-discovery*. Through experimentation, feedback, persistent practice, risk taking, failure, and success, we human beings continue to discover our interests, passions, potentials, aversions, values, styles, and tastes. At age 85, I am still discovering myself, with even greater and more critical insights than I had during those awkward, moody, youthful outbursts of my teenage years!

The human journey is also one of growing intelligence. Lauren B. Resnick (1999) of the University of Pittsburgh reminds us, "One's intelligence is the sum of one's *habits of mind*." It's true that if our goals for education include having students eager to pursue individual and unique passions, sustain innate curiosity, and work collaboratively to create solutions to complex problems, then they need teachers who can not only model but also coach the self-direction, persistence, and reflective problem solving that is characterized by interdependent, flexible, and creative thinking. The Habits of Mind drive, motivate, activate, and direct our intellectual capacities. This book provides a framework for personalized learning and a blueprint for instruction that requires an explicit focus on and assessment of the Habits of Mind. In weaving together these two significant bodies of educational knowledge, theory, and practice, the authors present a holistic model of schooling that is a more accurate reflection of our curious and extraordinary human nature.

And yet, for all we have in common, our differences cannot be denied. Because we know that every learner is unique and that no two brains are wired exactly alike, a shift from standardizing and averaging to personalizing just makes sense. The approach to education in this book equips students to pursue their interests and passions and removes compliance-focused strictures on both student and teacher creativity. It's about empowerment, about discovery and liberation, about recasting traditional roles, and about shifting our educational assumptions.

To that point, another consideration that drives this book is the futurist argument that teaching academics, although still necessary, may no longer be enough. As Andreas Schleicher, Director for the Directorate of Education and Skills for the Organisation for Economic Co-operation and development (OECD), notes, "The world economy no longer pays for what people know but for what they can do with what they know" (Big Think, 2014). Accordingly, the content and the disciplines that we traditionally teach must be reframed not only as outcomes but also as opportunities for experiencing, applying, and reflecting on essential dispositions represented in the Habits of Mind: persisting, remaining open to continuous learning, thinking interdependently, thinking flexibly, questioning and problem posing, and so on.

When the teaching of content is repositioned in this way, an array of new and powerful mental models become available. We realize that we must make personalized student self-evaluation as significant an influence as external evaluations have long been. We realize that if students graduate from our schools still dependent upon others to tell them when they are adequate, good, or excellent, then we've missed the whole point of what self-directed learning is about. We realize the value of using a feedback spiral as a planning tool and a guide for learning. In the pages ahead, you'll find many models and examples of teachers shifting the evaluative responsibility to students by co-creating with them an enhanced capacity for self-analysis, self-referencing, and self-modification.

In a sense, all educators are futurists in that we are trying to prepare students for both the present and the ambiguous future that does not yet exist. We need a shared vision of the skills and dispositions that facilitate success across and beyond defined subject areas—a vision that reflects a curriculum of *process* that will support mastery of any content and give students personal practice engaging with complex problems, dilemmas, and conflicts that have no clear or immediate resolution. You'll find this vision articulated in the pages ahead. And what is most significant about this vision is that it is as important for adults as it is for students.

—Arthur L. Costa
Granite Bay, California

Preface

Personalized learning. It has become a popular, even jargonized term. If asked, most educators could offer some explanation of what it means to "personalize learning." In all likelihood, these explanations would differ wildly.

In this book, we hope to contribute some clarity on what personalized learning is, what it can look like in the classroom, and all that it can help students achieve. Although we use the past-tense term *personalized*, we do not mean to imply that the work of personalization is ever truly "complete." It's an ongoing process, a paradigm shift to a learner-centered approach to teaching. We delve into not just what it means to personalize students' learning experiences and how educators can go about this but also why it matters so much that we do.

Our conclusions are based on considerable work in the field. We have the privilege of working with many educators who are struggling to give meaning to and respond to ever-changing targets. Standards: *Which ones are best?* Competencies: *Which ones to prioritize?* Assessments: *Which ones tell the most complete story of student progress and learning?* Legislators: *What story do they want to hear?* Parents: *What do they most want to know and need to know about their children's education?* Having observed how the shifting responses to those questions cause people to lose their way, we hope to provide a true north for educators—a set of values and a vision that will serve students well, both now and in the future.

In the first chapter, we clarify what we mean by true north, first positing that educators' most important work is to help students develop the intellectual and social strength of character they need to live well in the world and then offering our best conclusion on how to achieve this: by embracing a transformative, student-driven model of personalized learning built on the set of dispositions known as the Habits of Mind. In Chapter 2, we take a hard look at the practical work of making curriculum more student-driven, paying close attention to something that is fundamental to all learning: teacher–student relationships. In Chapter 3, we consider how the roles of teacher and student change as they co-create a set of goals and determine what will drive their inquiry process. In Chapter 4, mindful of the work of Grant Wiggins and Jay McTighe (1998, 2005), we explore the question *What do we want students to know and be able to do as a result of learning?* In Chapter 5, we focus on instruction, offering many examples of how to create a more independent and responsible classroom in which students are able to follow their interests with a commitment to deeper learning. In Chapter 6, we examine feedback as an excellent catalyst for continued growth. In our seventh and last chapter, we explore climate change—how to create the kind of culture for learning and thinking that transforms a classroom, a whole school, and an entire system into a personalized and student-driven learning environment.

Change does not come easily. It requires letting go of old habits and traditions and embracing a new mental model for this century and for the students we teach now. It means preparing these students for a world that is vastly different from the world that most of us were educated in. As Heidi Hayes Jacobs has reminded us,

> Schools are launching pads, launching our kids into their futures. Unfortunately, a lot of what we teach now looks identical to what we taught 40, 50, or 60 years ago. There's a need for both timeless curriculum content and timely content. What seems to be falling by the wayside is timely content. (Perkins-Gough, 2003/2004, p. 13)

Personalized learning with Habits of Mind offers an entry point to timely content and, at the same time, invites students to join with teachers in the search for timely problems and queries. It sparks innovation and imagination, and it empowers students to take responsible risks on behalf of their own passions and aspirations. It is a pathway to true success.

Empowering Students
to Find Their Own Way

The shift from industrialized to personalized is a global one, and it is revolutionizing medicine, journalism, music, television, publishing, politics, and self-expression. Yet in the school environment, life continues to be mostly standardized. We remain in a culture that promotes one curriculum for all, one age group and one grade at a time, and one set of tests to determine learning.

However, the fact is, the more challenging, complex, and uncertain the world becomes, the greater the need for education to transform our ways of customizing learning. We must encourage our students to become problem solvers and creative thinkers. If our students are to be successful, they will need to find work that is as satisfying to the human spirit as it is satisfying economically.

As teachers, we need to design learning experiences that help students get in touch with who they want to be and what they want to accomplish in the world. We must include opportunities for all students to build social capital and develop a voice for interaction with people in power positions. They must learn how to create and use professional networks and develop and promote their innovative ideas. Enter personalized learning.

Personalized learning is an umbrella term under which many practices fit, each designed to accelerate student learning by tailoring instruction to individuals' needs and skills as they go about fulfilling curricular requirements. We believe the scope of personalized learning, as it's presently and generally understood, must expand to allow students opportunities to explore and develop their own passions and interests. One of its aims must be to unleash the power of students' aspirations, which will strengthen their eventual participation in citizenship and the economy. As Tony Wagner and Ted Dintersmith (2015) have suggested, "The purpose of education is to engage students with their passions and growing sense of purpose, teach them critical skills needed for career and citizenship, and inspire them to do their very best to make their world better."

This purpose, however, often remains unfulfilled. Students from even the most privileged schools may suppress their aspirations—their passions and intense interests—because their deepest desires are held captive to the practicality of what others call success. Likewise, students born into poverty may suppress their aspirations because their teachers deem those aspirations impossible to achieve. The promotion of college and career readiness often creates more hurdles for students to overcome as they face the gatekeepers of their future. We believe that the way to help students build the intellectual and social strength of character that everyone needs in the contemporary world is by attending to the dispositions for continuous learning and success through personalized experiences.

In this chapter, we first describe what personalized learning truly is and can be and then turn our attention to the dispositions necessary to bring this model of schooling to life—the Habits of Mind. We show how the fusion of the two provides a framework for creating learning spaces in which students thoughtfully solve problems and invent their own ideas.

The Four Attributes of Personalized Learning

Personalized learning is a progressively student-driven model of education that empowers students to pursue aspirations, investigate problems, design solutions, chase curiosities, and create performances (Zmuda, Curtis, & Ullman, 2015). There are four defining attributes of personalized learning, each of which can be used as a filter to examine existing classroom practices or construct new ones. These are *voice*, *co-creation*, *social construction*, and *self-discovery*.

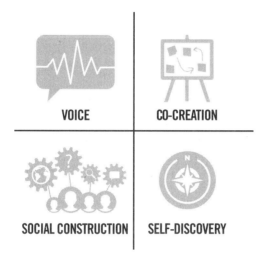

Voice

The first defining attribute is *voice*—the student's involvement and engagement in "the what" and "the how" of learning early in the learning process. Instead of being passengers on the curricular journey that the adults have mapped out, students are valued participants, helping to set the curricular agenda and taking the wheel themselves. Personalized learning encourages students to recognize not just the power of their own ideas but also how their ideas can shift and evolve through exposure to the ideas of others.

Co-Creation

The second attribute is *co-creation*. In personalized learning, students work with the teacher to develop a challenge, problem, or idea; to clarify what is being measured (learning goals); to envision the product or performance (assessment); and to outline an action plan that will result in an outcome that achieves the desired results (learning actions). Through the regular co-creation personalized learning requires, students flex and build their innovative and creative muscles.

Social Construction

The third attribute of personalized learning is ***social construction***, meaning that students build ideas through relationships with others as they theorize and investigate in pursuit of common learning goals. As one of us has written elsewhere, "Vygotsky (1978) refers to the social construction of knowledge—the idea that people learn through dialogue, discussion, building on one another's ideas. ... Teaching students to experience these processes help[s] learners to internalize and reshape, or transform, new information" (Kallick & Alcock, 2013, p. 51). There is real power in feeling that you are not alone, in the sense of camaraderie that comes from working collaboratively to effect a change, create a performance, or build a prototype. For students, the experience of individual bits of knowledge, ideas, and actions coalescing into a larger and better whole can be transformative, even magical.

Self-Discovery

The fourth defining attribute of personalized learning is ***self-discovery***—the process of students' coming to understand themselves as learners. They reflect on the development of ideas, skill sets, knowledge, and performances, and this helps them envision what might come next as well as what they might do next, explore next, create next. Our aim is for students to become self-directed learners who know how to manage themselves in a variety of situations. By helping them learn about themselves, we help them build the capacity to make wise decisions and navigate a turbulent and rapidly changing world.

A Pause for Clarification: How Do Individualization and Differentiation Differ from Personalized Learning?

When reflecting on the four attributes of personalized learning, some readers may connect them to other instructional models often referred to as "personalized"—specifically, *individualization* and *differentiation*. Although these models are similar to personalized learning in some respects, there are meaningful distinctions, particularly concerning the nature of the tasks and the level of control students have over the learning experience. Figure 1.1 (see p. 6) shows how the student's and teacher's roles evolve from model to model.

Individualization

Individualization, as with personalized learning, allows for instructional learning to happen anytime and anyplace. The blended learning approach is a well-known application of individualization. However, in individualization students are always *assigned* the learning tasks, and they go on to use technology, such as computer-adapted models, a software platform, or a teacher-generated playlist, to complete those tasks. Typically, the students control the pace of their learning experience on the road to demonstrating mastery of the material. They can replay videos, do practice problems, answer questions, and receive instant feedback on their work in preparation for a computer- or teacher-generated assessment.

Individualized learning is "personalized" in that it is a way to use the efficiencies of technology to adjust the assignment and pacing to reflect the needs of the learner. There might be an emphasis on students reflecting on their learning and deepening their understanding of how they learn best. However, the relational part of the learning may be overlooked.

FIGURE 1.1

The Evolving Roles of Student and Teacher in Three Instructional Models

MODEL	STUDENT'S ROLE	TEACHER'S ROLE	EXAMPLES
Personalized Learning	Actively pursues authentic, complex problems that inspire *co-creation* in the inquiry, analysis, and final product and incorporate opportunities for *voice, social construction*, and *self-discovery*.	Facilitates learning through questions, conferences, and feedback.	• Student develops playlists (curation of texts, experiences) • Student leads conferences • Student achieves mastery based on demonstrated ability and performance
Individualization	Controls the pace of the topic as well as when to demonstrate mastery.	Drives instruction through teacher-created tasks and related lesson plans.	• Teacher develops playlists • Khan Academy • Dreambox or Compass Learning
Differentiation	Selects from a range of content, process, or product options.	Tailors instruction based on individual student needs and preferences.	• Literature circles around different texts but on same theme • Student contracts • Choice boards

Source: From *Learning Personalized: The Evolution of the Contemporary Classroom* (pp. 10–11), by A. Zmuda, G. Curtis, & D. Ullman, 2015, San Francisco: Jossey-Bass. Copyright 2015 by Jossey-Bass. Adapted with permission.

With a blended learning approach, students may complete some of the work independently using technology. They may co-create projects in which they apply what they are learning in an experiential environment. They may also work with a group. The significant distinction of blended learning is not how much students do off site and how much they do on site. Rather, it is about how much *say* the students have in the work they are doing.

A ***personalized learning model*** involves students in the design and development of the tasks they engage in. There has been much talk about technology forcing "disruption" in the schools, but in our opinion, what technology is disrupting is an exclusively compliance-driven school. This is a welcome development. Engagement is not measured by how quickly a student races through the material; it comes from how relevant, interesting, and worthy the student finds the material. This kind of engagement is built into personalized learning, as the students themselves identify or create an idea, question, or problem; determine key actions, resources, and timelines; engage in an iterative cycle of drafts; receive and reflect on feedback; and pursue next steps until the task is completed. The teacher's role is to work with students to hone skills and acquire knowledge; to give that knowledge context; and to help students ground knowledge and skill development in authentic, complex, and problem-based endeavors.

Differentiation

Differentiation embraces the reality of all the learners in the room, with their range of skills, readiness levels, and areas of interest. In this model, teachers start where the students are to create a range of learning experiences that students can be assigned to or select themselves. It's the latter form of differentiation—when students exercise choice—that can be confused with personalization, situations in which students can select the resources or topics to explore (content differentiation); how to investigate or develop an idea (process differentiation); and the form of the demonstration of learning will take (product differentiation). This differentiation encourages student choice within the confines of what the teacher has developed as viable options. The teacher is still in control of the design and management of the experience.

In comparison, ***a personalized learning model*** opens up the door for students to significantly shape what they do and how they demonstrate learning. They have a seat at the design table, the evaluation table, and the exhibition table. They have more ownership from start to finish around the development of an idea, the investigation, the analysis, the refinement, and the presentation to an authentic audience.

Readers who are familiar with project-based learning might like to see it included for comparison in Figure 1.1. However, we see project-based learning as something that is under the umbrella of personalized learning. It is part of that progression in which students move from developing their thinking as part of a teacher-designed set of choices for a project to developing a project based on an independent, personal inquiry of their own. Project-based learning always includes a challenging problem or question, sustained inquiry, authenticity, student voice and choice, reflection, critique and revision, and a public product (Larmer, Mergendoller, & Boss, 2015). These experiences can be vetted by examining them for *voice, co-creation, social construction,* and *self-discovery*—in other words, by using the four attributes of personalized learning as filters to clarify the degree to which students have opportunities to think, create, share, and discover.

The student-centered personalized learning we explore in this book is a vibrant, dynamic, messy way of learning that breaks down the walls that separate subject areas into silos, the school world from the outside world, and individual achievement from community growth. Students learn from and are influenced by the adults, peers, and experts with whom they work as they socially construct knowledge. They use what they learn about themselves as a compass to direct their choices, decisions, and active engagement.

Frankly, this is demanding work. How can teachers equip their students to meet the challenge?

Habits of Mind—A Set of Dispositions for Engagement and Learning

If we want students to reach for higher levels of thinking and performing, they must have opportunities to engage in, develop, and demonstrate a much richer set of skills and dispositions than are measured in the narrowly defined tests so prevalent today. The emphasis of most standards-based tests is measuring and reporting on academic knowledge. Although that is important, our students need to build the habits necessary to embark on projects in which the outcome is not immediately apparent. They need to develop the Habits of Mind that direct their strategic abilities and expand their resourcefulness and capacity for engaging with and solving challenging problems.

A habit is something done automatically, without too much self-awareness. Consider driving a car, for example. Although there is a certain amount of automaticity in steering, accelerating, breaking, passing, and merging once someone has learned how to drive, a driver needs mindfulness when confronted with a disruption, such as an icy road or a pothole. These environmental disruptions demand considered decisions. Likewise, students often go "on automatic," memorizing what is expected on a test. However, when they encounter a situation of uncertainty, a situation in which the answer is not immediately apparent, they need to be more considered in their thought processes. As Habits of Mind, such as thinking flexibly or questioning and problem posing, are brought to consciousness, students are able to confidently navigate the complexity of the situation. The Habits reside in that very important space in which we shift from automaticity to mindfulness.

The 16 Habits of Mind (Costa & Kallick, 2008), shown in Figure 1.2 (see p. 10), are drawn from a modern view of intelligence that casts off traditional abilities-centered theories and replaces them with a growth mindset. These habits are often called "soft skills" or "noncognitive skills"—terminology that suggests something easy. In fact,

FIGURE 1.2
The 16 Habits of Mind

Persisting: *Stick to it!* Persevering in task through to completion; remaining focused.	**Managing impulsivity:** *Take your time!* Thinking before acting; remaining calm, thoughtful, and deliberative.
Listening with understanding and empathy: *Understand others!* Devoting mental energy to another person's thoughts and ideas; holding in abeyance one's own thoughts in order to perceive another's point of view and emotions.	**Thinking flexibly:** *Look at it another way!* Being able to change perspectives, generate alternatives, consider options.
Thinking about your thinking (metacognition): *Know your knowing!* Being aware of one's own thoughts, strategies, feelings, and actions and their effects on others.	**Striving for accuracy and precision:** *Check it again!* Seeking exactness, fidelity, and craftsmanship.
Questioning and problem posing: *How do you know?* Having a questioning attitude; knowing what data are needed and developing questioning strategies to produce those data.	**Applying past knowledge to novel situations:** *Use what you learn!* Accessing prior knowledge; transferring knowledge beyond the situation in which it was learned.
Thinking and communicating with clarity and precision: *Be clear!* Striving for accurate communication in both written and oral form; avoiding overgeneralizations, distortions, and deletions.	**Gathering data through all senses:** *Use your natural pathways!* Gathering data through all the sensory pathways—gustatory, olfactory, tactile, kinesthetic, auditory, and visual.
Creating, imagining, and innovating: *Try a different way!* Generating new and novel ideas, striving for fluency and originality.	**Responding with wonderment and awe:** *Have fun figuring it out!* Finding the world awesome and mysterious and being intrigued with phenomena and beauty.
Taking responsible risks: *Venture out!* Being adventuresome; living on the edge of one's competence.	**Finding humor:** *Laugh a little!* Finding the whimsical, incongruous, and unexpected; being able to laugh at oneself.
Thinking interdependently: *Work together!* Being able to work with and learn from others in reciprocal situations.	**Remaining open to continuous learning:** *Learn from experiences!* Having humility and pride when admitting we don't know; resisting complacency.

Source: Adapted from *Habits of Mind Across the Curriculum: Practical and Creative Strategies for Teachers* (p. X), edited by A. Costa and B. Kallick, 2009, Alexandria, VA: ASCD. Copyright 2009 by ASCD.

these skills are among the most difficult to develop because they require a great deal of cognitive consciousness. Ultimately, they become an internal compass that answers the question "What is the most *thought-full* thing that I can do right now?" As the classroom and school focus on the four attributes—*voice, co-creation, social construction*, and *self-discovery*—the Habits of Mind become a set of behaviors that students and teachers build on, come to value in themselves and others, and ultimately use to navigate the complexities they face both inside and beyond school.

As teachers and students develop fluency with the Habits of Mind, they don't have to always remind themselves about which habit is called for in a given situation. As with any habit, practice strengthens the likelihood that the person will use it without needing a reminder. For example, when students are given the opportunity to pursue a project, they develop their "mind muscles" by creating, imagining, and innovating. They become more fluent as they work together and learn how to think more flexibly, remaining open to one another's ideas. They are able to sharpen the research they will do by questioning and problem posing. As they search the web for "how to" material, they will need to use precise language.

Foremost in this process, students and teachers persist in the face of uncertainty. Individuals who have adopted Habits of Mind as a way of being *thought-full* about life are more aware of and focused on the skills that affect their success. Similarly, schools that adopt the Habits of Mind as a part of their vision become learning communities in which all members—students, teachers, administrators, parents, and community members—act with care and thought.

Personalized Learning with Habits of Mind

Personalized learning with Habits of Mind facilitate a more holistic approach to learning. *If* we want our students to pursue aspirations, investigate problems, design solutions, chase curiosities, and create performances, *then* they need opportunities to engage with and in meaningful problems and challenges and coaching in habits such as thinking flexibly, listening with understanding and empathy, and questioning and problem posing. In other words, personalized learning is the organizational frame we need—the pedagogical structure that requires students to use the explicit thinking behaviors captured in the Habits of Mind.

Moving in this direction requires teachers and students to think differently and commit to a new process for learning. Let's take a look at the are four key shifts in thinking that characterize personalized learning with Habits of Mind

Learning Is Teacher Led *and* Student Directed

The power of a teacher-determined curriculum ensures there is an agreed-upon set of goals and assessments that each student will experience. This curricular guide can be locally designed, implemented, monitored, and refined to evaluate the impact on student learning. Personalized learning means that students are invited to assume ownership of this guide by co-creating their tasks, projects, and assessments.

Some students may be unwilling or unexcited to have a voice in their own learning. Student apathy cannot be allowed to overwhelm potential engagement. It's true that many students feel disengaged by the teacher-identified problems, challenges, or texts they're expected to complete; our task is to teach them how to persist, apply past knowledge to new situations, and think about their thinking. This promotes self-management and a commitment to keep working toward a desired performance.

Students Build Disciplinary Knowledge *and* Cross-Disciplinary Skills

Discipline-specific organizations, such as the National Science Teachers Association and National Art Education Association, articulate key concepts, knowledge, and skills that anchor their discipline, periodically reviewing and refining their expectations to ensure those expectations are feasible, are up to date, and include broader perspectives. Other organizations, such as the Partnership for 21st Century Skills and the National Governors Association for Best Practices, contend the focus of learning should be on the growth of cross-disciplinary skills.

The more we learn about personalized learning performances, the more we realize that discipline-specific goals, while important, are woefully insufficient if we want students to thrive in contemporary society. For example, instead of reading about what an engineer does and answering straightforward questions on the role of an engineer, students can leverage critical thinking and problem solving to create, imagine, and innovate by using the Engineering Design Process in combination with their courses in the arts. Instead of researching a current global conflict and reporting on their findings, students can use interview skills learned in English class to seek out and interview people affected by the conflict, demonstrating empathy for their plight and comparing how these person-centered views contrast with portrayals in the global media.

Student Learning Requires Disciplinary Knowledge *and* Dispositional Thinking

The teaching of disciplinary knowledge and dispositional thinking are complementary, not competing, aims. When schools include Habits of Mind as an intentional component of practice, they are acknowledging that teaching for thinking is as important as teaching content knowledge. Their curriculum, instruction, and assessment intentionally address how to think critically and creatively and how to problem-solve.

Consider that when a student is thinking creatively, he or she engages in at least two Habits of Mind: (1) *taking a responsible risk*, and (2) *creating, imagining, and innovating*. These habits can be deconstructed into a set of teachable behaviors. The teacher's role is to continually model and use the Habits of Mind to draw out the best of the student's thinking. The student's role is to use—and further develop through use—the Habits of Mind needed to fully experience a self-directed performance. Not only should the level of cognition remain high in terms of the learning and the performance, but also the level of metacognition should bring about a consciousness and an intention concerning decisions about where and when to use the habits for effective thinking.

Standards Can Offer the Freedom to Create

As educators, we can and should agree on common aims of schooling that are aligned with standards, but we should also honor the values and aspirations of the community we serve. By designing broader goals and associated competencies to measure progress, we invite students to create and pursue inquiries and ideas. Teacher and student can work together to identify how a personalized design aligns with learning goals as well as to discuss resources and actions. For example, teachers in North Carolina's Charlotte-Mecklenburg school district came together and created their own personalized learning profiles, adapted from Habits of Mind (see Figure 1.3). While teachers in the district use the dispositions differently—for example, in morning meetings or in project-based learning—the district as a whole is creating common language around the dispositions for grades K–12.

To Sum Up

We must move toward schools that offer students more choices as they learn how to fully develop their **voice**, hone their capacities to **co-create**, and explore the benefits of **social construction** and **self-discovery**.

Teachers frequently ask if personalizing learning means that every student will be doing something different. What we are suggesting is that these kinds of interest-based experiences be offered as an additional opportunity for learning—more ways in which students will develop academic and dispositional competencies as they struggle through the process of innovating and inventing. So yes, when teachers provide these opportunities, it is likely that there will be many different projects going on simultaneously in the class. The choices that students make will be based on their curiosity and their interests.

FIGURE 1.3
Personalized Learning Profiles in Charlotte-Mecklenburg Schools

Personalized Learning: Learner Profile

cms®
Charlotte-Mecklenburg Schools

PersonalizedLearning

Personalized Learning in Charlotte-Mecklenburg Schools aims to develop the whole child and empower them to take ownership of their learning by providing them with multiple pathways to demonstrate mastery learning in order to be successful and productive 21st century citizens in an ever-changing world.

Personalized Learning scholars strive to be...

 Creative & Critical Thinkers: I think before I act. I routinely examine problems in new ways and seek to find creative solutions. My imagination allows me to express myself and develop new ideas. I use the design process to help guide my thinking.

 Effective Communicators: I clearly convey my thoughts, questions, solutions, and ideas in multiple ways, including verbally, written, and digitally.

 Collaborators: I effectively work with others to reach our goals—combining our talents, expertise, and smarts. I actively listen to others' ideas and contribute my own, which allows me to function as part of a team.

 Entrepreneurs: I think differently and am resilient in my quest to be innovative. I persevere through difficult tasks. I identify needs or challenges and proactively find solutions to address those needs.

 Flexible & Adaptable: I can adapt to change. I am able to work effectively in a variety of environments. I value other people's strengths and learn from them.

Receptive & Reflective to Feedback: I value feedback to help myself improve and further develop my skills to achieve personal growth. Reflecting critically about past experiences helps me to inform my future progress. I am aware of my own strategies, feelings, actions and their effects on others.

 Leaders: I do the right thing, even when no one is looking. I empower and support those around me. I am constantly finding ways to improve myself. I maintain a positive attitude and a sense of humor.

 Open-Minded: I am willing to consider and listen to new ideas and understand my first assumptions might not be accurate. I am respectful, objective and am able to see things from multiple perspectives.

 Self-Directed Learners: I manage my goals and time, am able to work independently, and take initiative to advance my skill levels. I am committed to learning as a lifelong process. I take pride in my work.

 Academic Risk Takers: I am driven, determined, and willingly accept new and difficult challenges. I am resourceful and view mistakes and failures as opportunities to learn and grow.

cms®
Charlotte-Mecklenburg Schools

Every Child. Every Day. For a Better Tomorrow.

Source: Charlotte-Mecklenburg Schools, Charlotte, NC. Used with permission.

Personalized learning with Habits of Mind is a departure from the traditional interactions in which the teacher has a clearly defined curricular agenda—even in cases where that curricular agenda offers students creative options for fulfilling the requirements. When students are trusted to find their own way, teachers and students interact with one another differently. The experience of school and of learning is different—and better. We'll explore this experience in the chapters ahead.

Toward a More
Student-Driven Practice

A student-driven model of personalized learning attends to the human architecture—to how teachers and students interact with one another. In this chapter, we begin looking at how teachers can rework the curriculum for effective personalization and, at the same time, reframe *their* work in order to be a partner for students, who assume a more central role.

For teachers looking to create a learning community that provides opportunities for *voice, co-creation, social construction,* and *self-discovery,* there are seven key elements to address:

1. Goals
2. Inquiry/idea generation
3. Task and audience
4. Evaluation
5. Cumulative demonstration of learning
6. Instructional plan
7. Feedback

These elements were delineated as critical concerns in *Learning Personalized* (Zmuda et al., 2015), and we continue to expand our understanding of them based on ongoing analysis and inspiration from the field. It's by making shifts in these seven elements—

by altering the roles that teachers and students take on—that a person-alized learning environment takes root and begins to thrive.

We will explore each of these elements in the chapters to come, discussing and illustrating necessary shifts, highlighting the Habits of Mind that the new approaches require and help to develop, and providing tools and recommendations for adjusting classroom prac-tice. (For a full summary of these elements, teacher and student roles in each, and the related Habits of Mind, see the Appendix.) Each ele-ment is followed by a reflective question for the lesson designer and a description of the impact it has on the roles of student and teacher. Finally, we suggest related Habits of Mind that might be explicitly enlisted as part of the process of developing personalized learning.

First, though, we want to take some time to provide an overview of the seven elements—introducing you to what they look like within a personalized learning environment and calling out how each pro-vides opportunities for *voice, co-creation, social construction*, and *self-discovery.*

Element 1: Goals

What are the desired results?
As educators, we know the benefits of beginning with the end in mind and planning on the basis of what we want students to know, be able to do, and understand. In a personalized learning environ-ment, students and teachers work together to identify both appro-priate subject-specific and cross-disciplinary **goals** (e.g., critical thinking, collaboration, creativity) and dispositional goals (e.g., managing impulsivity, listening with understanding and empathy) that are appropriate, given the topic, the time available, and each student's aspirations.

The subject-specific and cross-disciplinary goals are aligned to state and national standards and written in clear and accessible language so both students and teachers can identify priorities as well as understand the goals' significance to the performance or product.

For example, New York's North Rockland Central School District identified teacher-framed goals and student-framed goals about "doing science" that are aligned with the Next Generation Science Standards as well as with the Common Core State Standards for English Language Arts and for Mathematical Practice. Figure 2.1 displays how three of those goals look from both the teacher and student perspectives.

FIGURE 2.1

Teacher- and Student-Framed Disciplinary Goals

DISCIPLINARY GOALS (TEACHER)	DISCIPLINARY GOALS (STUDENT)	RELATED STANDARDS
Ask questions to define a problem and develop ideas for an investigation.	I can ask questions before and after doing a fair test (that is, an experiment that is carefully controlled) or designing a model.	NGSS: K–5 Practice 1, K–2-ETS1-1, 3–5-ETS1-1 CCSS ELA: RI.1, SL.1 CCSS MP: 1
Observe and explore a given system or concept to deepen scientific understanding.	I can make observations to help me understand _____ (fill in with a particular system or concept).	NGSS: K–5 Practice 6, K–2-ETS1-1, 3–5-ETS1-1 CCSS ELA: RI.3, RI.7, W.7
Plan and conduct an investigation to test a hypothesis using precise collection, recording, and safety practices.	I can plan and carry out a fair test with my partner(s) to collect and record data.	NGSS: K–5 Practice 3, K–5 Practice 5, K–2-ETS1-1, 3–5-ETS1-3 CCSS MP: 1, 2, 4, 5, 6

Source: North Rockland Central School District, NY. Used with permission.

Asking students to articulate goals gives them the opportunity to exercise their *voice*. Their perspective becomes central to the way they will approach the performance or product and shapes the vision of what they hope to accomplish. Students *co-create* goals when they think aloud with the teacher about what they will work to achieve and contemplate what might help them become more skillful, adaptive, and "thought-full." It's when students pay attention to these priorities that they uncover areas of strength and areas of discomfort; this is essential to *self-discovery*. Acquiring this insight also puts them in the position to reach out to others for guidance, support, or feedback (*social construction*).

Element 2: Inquiry/Idea Generation

What aspect of the topic sparks your thinking? What is worth pursuing? Creating a personalized learning environment calls for a clear shift from a standardized, teacher-designed (or software-generated) learning experience to one that is distinctly shaped by students. The goal is for students to assume responsibility for their exploration of the curriculum. They isolate aspects of topics that resonate with them and that they want to know more about. They articulate not just particular problems or ideas to investigate but also how they will structure this investigation. To do this, they must engage in such Habits of Mind as *questioning and problem posing* to uncover root causes, *thinking flexibly* as they evaluate multiple perspectives, and *thinking about their thinking* as they develop a course of action to pursue. Consider these examples:

• *Science fair project*: Students control the topic, design of the investigation, and related artifacts. They must consider clarity of the research question; appropriateness of the design and methodology; accuracy of the data collection, analysis, and conclusions; quality of the presentation; creativity; perseverance; and clear and precise communication.

• *"Standing on a soapbox" speech*: Students advocate for a community issue they feel passionately about, clarifying the problem or need, offering compelling anecdotes and research, and inspiring others to act. They must consider the quality of their spoken text (ideas and content, organization, language, delivery); think flexibly to show consideration of multiple perspectives; and pay attention to the listeners' level of engagement.

• *Health matters*: Students investigate a health concern that matters to them or their loved ones and develop an informed statement. They must consider the clarity of their core issue or concern, the credibility of their sources and the accuracy of information presented, and the persuasiveness of the appeal for the target audience. They must also be prepared to create, imagine, and innovate their way to possible alternatives. During their investigation, they also need to gather data with all the senses, as when considering what the condition feels and what it looks like.

When students are invited to the design table for **inquiry/idea generation**, they can use their *voice* to offer their point of view and talk through biases and misunderstandings, identify areas of personal disconnection, and suggest ideas for further research and learning. They assume the role of a partner in instructional design, which represents a big change from the typical classroom hierarchy and dynamics.

Students *co-create* by developing an approach to pursue an idea or an inquiry while working within task parameters (e.g., historical research, creation of a short story, demonstration of quadratic functions). Doing so calls on the habit of *questioning and problem posing. Social construction* occurs as students seek out information, ideas, and perspectives to guide task development—by consulting experts or peers who have intimate knowledge of the topic and using others as a sounding board to work through ideas or roadblocks. They are developing the habit of *gathering data using all the senses.*

Self-discovery comes about as students uncover how they navigate through the challenges they've set for themselves: how they start making sense of a problem or how they generate an idea, how they handle the frustration of not getting it quite right for the umpteenth time, how they work through revisions or dead ends by analyzing what happened. They are *reflecting on what they are learning* and *responding with wonderment and awe* as they recognize that they are *remaining open to continuous learning.*

Element 3: Task and Audience

How does audience shape creation and communication?
Personalizing learning calls for expanding students' opportunity to share information, ideas, and performances with authentic audiences

beyond the teacher. Development of **task and audience** often go hand in hand, and tasks have natural real-world audiences. Yes, asking students to enter competitions or include their work in public exhibitions is one way to find an authentic audience, but it's not strictly necessary. They can realize many of the same benefits by consulting the criteria for these events, working with teachers to find community members with the requisite evaluative expertise, and enlisting these people as audience members. Having students work to criteria established outside of the classroom, such as industry standards or judging criteria for competitions, makes learning feel more meaningful and engaging. Consider these examples:

• *Culinary arts program*: Students earn industry credentials in ServSafe, a food and beverage safety training and certificate program administered by the National Restaurant Association; master basic kitchen safety and health standards in a state health department-inspected kitchen; and run a working restaurant and catering business with cash customers.

• *Star Trek Replicator Challenge* (www.futureengineers.org/startrek): Students help astronauts "live long and prosper" on future deep-space exploration missions by creating 3-D printed designs for materials that will help crews eat nutritious meals in the year 2050. Possible designs include hardware needed to grow and harvest plants and hardware needed to prepare, eat, and dispose of food. Criteria include a 3–D printable model in a 6-inch by 6-inch by 6-inch printer volume; hardware designed for Earth's moon, another planet, or another planet's moon; hardware that advances long-term human space exploration; and hardware that is designed to be printed with one nonedible printing material (feedstock) of the student's choice. The feedstock can exist today or can be a theoretical future feedstock.

• *Youth Journalism* (http://youthjournalism.org): Open to students from 12 to 22 years old, this reporter-driven system encourages students to develop an idea and work to refine the story, with an emphasis on good writing and journalistic principles. Students delve into issues that matter to them, from covering the Arab Spring to exploring attitudes toward rape in India to examining school shootings in the United States to interviewing the Dalai Lama.

When students produce work for a broader audience, they have the chance to use *voice, co-creation*, and *social construction* to refine their sense of what is valuable by reflecting on similar circumstances and interviewing target audience members. They can consider others' points of view and debrief in groups to verify what did and didn't work. They also gain valuable experience communicating with purpose, versatility, clarity, and precision.

Self-discovery grows as students publish, perform, or broadcast their work. To move from the relative safety of "teacher as audience" to the uncertainty of "world as audience" requires confidence in the design, development, and delivery stages of a project. In taking these steps, students build the habit of *taking responsible risks*. For many, presenting their schoolwork to a wide audience feels like a huge risk; comfort with sharing their personal lives on social media often does not translate to sharing their solutions to a problem, their predictions from researching and analyzing data, or their creations based on an artistic form or genre.

Element 4: Evaluation

How is performance evaluated on a given task using criteria?
Personalized learning calls for a move away from teacher as sole judge of student work and toward a much greater use of self-assessment, particularly as the first stage of **evaluation**. After students self-assess, they take their findings to a conference with one or more evaluators, and the parties see how closely their evaluations of the work match. They make judgments using established criteria.

As noted in the previous section, using criteria identified by an outside organization or modeled on real-world standards (e.g., competition rules, manuscript requirements, industry standards) helps to give tasks authenticity. Here are two examples:

• An art teacher designs a *hallway gallery* where each student is expected to display a piece of work and write an artistic statement providing context for the idea, techniques used, and connection to the overall theme.

• An English language arts teacher assigns students to *write a short story*, borrowing criteria from another competition: The work must be original unpublished fiction, typed and double-spaced, and no more than 3,500 words. (See the Lorian Hemingway Short Story Competition at http://shortstorycompetition .com/guidelines.)

Alternatively, students themselves can play a role in drafting or revising evaluation criteria. Doing so typically gives them a stronger understanding of what is expected and how to reach certain benchmarks. Students and teacher can work together to produce a set of criteria that is both aspirational and rigorous by looking at curriculum standards as well as powerful examples and non-examples.

Evaluation requires students to demonstrate *voice* and *social construction* because they have a more meaningful role in the examination of work, and they conference with the teacher to identify areas of success and improvement. Students can use *co-creation* as they develop established criteria and related rubrics and evaluate others' work. Evaluation promotes *self-discovery* as students are called on to accurately describe the strengths and limitations of their performance.

Element 5: Cumulative Demonstration of Learning

How do we show evidence of learning over time?
The necessary transition here is from a scoring system that demonstrates achievement based on accumulation of grades to one that is portfolio based and asks students to focus on their growth over time. The advent of cost-effective learner management systems that can archive student work and report on student learning has changed how we capture and communicate long-term achievement and progress.

In personalized learning, students assume responsibility for collecting and then curating their own work to identify areas of strength and areas for growth, based on the desired outcomes. They then share that work with an audience (e.g., a teacher, a student-selected panel). Teachers can report on student achievement collectively or individually at intervals personalized by the student (e.g., when a project is complete rather than by artificially segmenting the year into *x* number of weeks). The portfolio-based system can include traditional grades or be an indicator of competencies met.

When students have an elevated role in the **cumulative demonstration of learning**, they use *voice* and *self-discovery* to articulate areas of frustration and insight. They use *co-creation* to develop a summary of performance that is based on supporting evidence from various artifacts (e.g., a finished design, a question-driven research plan, a team report on the quality of collaboration). And they work in conjunction with teachers to *socially construct* areas of improvement to further develop in the next unit or topic.

Element 6: Instructional Plan

What does designing a learning plan look like?
To personalize the instructional plan is to move from a situation in which the teacher is sole manager of learning to one in which students increasingly negotiate when, what, and with whom they are learning. A typical class period might have a range of teaching and learning opportunities, including guided instruction; self-navigated, technology-assisted instruction; teamwork; and 1:1 conference sessions with a peer, an expert, or the teacher. As teachers become more comfortable with relaxing their grip on instruction, students have a greater opportunity to advocate for and even determine its sequence, pace, and content.

Instruction in a personalized learning classroom has learning spaces dedicated to attending to student needs. Futurist and philosopher David Thornburg (2004) has described three learning spaces that have been used for thousands of years:

- *Campfire:* Learning from an expert or a storyteller in a more formal setting
  - *Watering hole:* Small-group discourse and collaborations
  - *Cave:* Individual study, reflection, and development

Each of these spaces facilitates the development of student-driven tasks. Collectively, they incorporate the four attributes of personalization that we have discussed and provide the opportunity to use and develop several Habits of Mind. The "campfire" is *social construction*, an opportunity to learn from others through *questioning and problem posing*, offering connections, and so forth. The "watering hole" helps build *voice* and *co-creation*; the small group allows for more extensive *thinking interdependently* as members collaborate and share ideas. The "cave" is well suited to *self-discovery* and *co-creation* as students have an opportunity to examine their work and develop ideas.

The goal of the **instructional plan** becomes empowering students to be self-directed. Rather than obliging them to ask permission to access resources, they learn to use those resources respectfully and responsibly to get the information and experience they need. They learn to *listen with understanding* as they reach out to cultures beyond their everyday experiences. Here are some examples:

- Students work through a series of messy mathematics problems in any order they want to demonstrate their ability to solve polynomial equations and inequalities. They can seek assistance from all kinds of resources, including but not limited to peers, math websites, and the teacher.
- A student engages in a conversation with a local architect via Skype to elicit feedback on maximizing square footage within a "tiny house." The two discuss stealth kitchens, transforming tables, wall beds, and other clever concepts that allow multiple uses of space.
- Students in a combined U.S. history and American literature class are asked to identify and explain a significant injustice and support that explanation with a range of sources. Students can work in small groups or individually to research how far back the injustice dates.

• Students use the reading comprehension—adaptive program Front Row (www.frontrowed.com) to improve their ability to comprehend text at various complexity levels. Articles, browsable by topic, are available in five different reading levels, and the teacher can assign articles to individual students based on the student's reading level. As students answer the reading comprehension questions correctly, their reading level increases. They continue to practice their skills by engaging in independent reading selections of their choice.

Element 7: Feedback

How does feedback promote growth?
Transitioning to a personalized learning environment calls for going from a situation in which the teacher is sole provider of **feedback** based on expected checkpoints to one in which students ask for feedback at natural stopping points—for example, when they have completed an initial draft, uncovered a thorny problem, or polished an idea and want to see its impact. To provide helpful feedback, both teacher and student need a common understanding of the criteria and must be able to describe the quality of the performance so far in relation to those criteria. The aim is to build the habit of *remaining open to continuous learning.*

Ideally, the student

• Frames the conversation by posing questions or concerns or by signaling one or two areas that he or she would most like feedback on.

• Listens intently by taking notes and asking follow-up questions to better understand the feedback.

• Thanks the person for his or her time and attention to the work.

• Determines the appropriate next steps and takes action, either individually or with the person giving feedback.

The person giving feedback

• Listens to the student with understanding and empathy.

- Focuses on offering positive, constructive, descriptive comments.
- Uses the criteria that have been established for assessing the project.
- Checks for student understanding of the feedback.
- Thanks the student for inviting the feedback session and helps set goals for the work that follows.

When students engage in giving and receiving feedback, their *voice* matters. By asking questions about the feedback they receive, they can focus the conversation on what would be most helpful to them. It's an iterative process; as students gain experience being on the receiving end of feedback, they grow more mindful of how to frame concerns or questions in a "thought-full" way and become better feedback givers themselves.

Engaging in feedback conversations involves both *co-creation* and *social construction*; students design their next step as a result of the experience. They also learn to be more adept at separating the work to be evaluated from the person who created it; this promotes *self-discovery*, along with the ability to navigate through uncomfortable conversations, offer candid and actionable feedback, and take next steps after the conversation is over.

A Teacher Reflects on Personalized Learning

We are all aware of the need to rethink the system so it can be more dynamic and more responsive to a new kind of learner. It's natural to be uncertain about this kind of change, however. When we spoke with high school biology teacher Craig Gastauer, he shared this reflection:

> Throughout my 20+ years of teaching, I have struggled to help *all* students learn deeply. Sure, a large number succeed, but I cannot allow myself to be satisfied with that. Some students succeeded because they learned (and learned very well) how to play the game of school. Some succeeded because of hard work. Yet others slipped through the cracks, and, with shame, I must admit that I allowed it.

Regardless of the group, I need to do a better job. Learning in my classroom must not happen by accident or happen because students are good at the game. I must help them learn to shift their learning process—from studying content out of context to examining issues, identifying problems, brainstorming potential solutions, and acting on their thoughts, and from mechanically trying to memorize content knowledge and skills to actively applying and building knowledge within the identified issues, problems, solutions, and actions.

We see the Habits of Mind as an explicit language that describes behaviors and strategies for intentionally working in thoughtful ways. They are the dispositions of effective thinkers—people who can learn from past experience, communicate their ideas with clarity, listen to others, and open themselves up to being influenced by others' ideas.

To Sum Up

To personalize learning is to place the learner at the center of curriculum; each of the seven key elements we have introduced represents a place for a teacher to make a conscious choice to move closer to a classroom that empowers the learner to be a significant part of the instructional design process. The four attributes of personalized learning—*voice, co-creation, social construction*, and *self-discovery*—serve as reminders of the key characteristics to seek. Filtering our current practices through these attributes gives us an idea of where we stand and the work that lies before us.

To clarify the degree to which your practice is already personalized—or moving in that direction—reflect on the seven elements we've discussed in this chapter and ask yourself the following questions:

 Voice: Do you offer students an opportunity to voice their questions, concerns, or deeper thinking about the content of their work? Do you encourage them to interact with others as they respectfully agree or disagree with them? Do students see themselves as citizens in the learning spaces they inhabit?

 Co-creation: Do you include students in designing the work they are engaging in? Do they actively shape their own goals, assessments, content, and performance choices as co-designers with teachers and other experts in the field?

 Social construction: Do students use the resourcefulness of others to give deeper meaning to their work? Do they interact with others who have more expertise in the field they are studying? Are they learning how to collaborate with others to influence and improve their own thinking?

 Self-discovery: Are students learning who they are as actively engaged learners? Are they reflecting on what they learn and understanding how to transfer that learning to new situations? Are they aware of their learning styles and the varying learning styles of others? Are they becoming more strategic about how they plan for, process, create, and produce new ways of demonstrating their learning?

Beginning with the End in Mind

Goals and Inquiry/Idea Generation

This chapter takes a closer look at the first two elements to consider when personalizing learning—setting **goals** and establishing the direction of the project through **inquiry and idea generation**.

These elements are naturally intertwined. Typically, for a given unit, teachers clarify what they want students to know, be able to do, and understand, and they develop goals and competencies focused on grade-level expectations that are often granular in nature. But the ideal way to approach the learning experience is through *uncoverage*. Teachers should be asking what broader questions and problems can help students delve into the content, look for generalizations and insights, and apply learning to novel situations. These are the kinds of goals that teachers need to establish in conjunction with students as the starting point for the backward design process.

Originally framed by Grant Wiggins and Jay McTighe (1998, 2005) in *Understanding by Design*, the backward design model is as powerful for students as it is for educators. Because students may not be accustomed to setting their own goals and determining their own direction for further study, beginning the process can be puzzling. Here, teachers play an important role as guides. They need to help students discover nuggets of gold in the curriculum. They need to offer a balance of guidance without taking over the direction.

Goals: Deciding on the Destination

Key Element	Role of the Student and the Teacher	Related Habits of Mind
GOALS *What are the desired results?*	Student and teacher identify how the topic aligns to goals (can be subject-specific, cross-disciplinary, or dispositional).	• Thinking about your thinking • Striving for accuracy • Thinking interdependently

In recent years, we have seen more educators embrace an *output-driven lesson design*, which is one that has transparency concerning what students should know and be able to do, multiple pathways for students to demonstrate achievement, and time as a variable to give students the opportunity to achieve, regardless of their past experience or skill set.

This is not a wholly new idea; the same approach can be found in outcome-based education and in vocational education programs tied to industry standards. What *is* new is the vision of how goals or competencies, personalized learning, and Habits of Mind can combine to create a more effective and thoughtful learning experience. When Habits of Mind are embedded in the learning design rather than considered an add-on, they promote more rigorous thinking. For example, when students are communicating with clarity and precision or creating, imagining, and innovating, they become more aware of and can elevate their thinking to higher levels.

Goals, Competencies, and Standards: What's the Difference?

Because this is no time to get lost in a sea of vocabulary, we want to pause to review some key definitions. The first distinction we want to make is between *standards* and *competencies*. Standards refer to what students are expected to know and be able to do at specific points within an educational program. They are developed at a state, province, or national level by a broad range of faculty, including folks from postsecondary institutions. Competencies, in contrast, are desired abilities, skills, or dispositions that students should learn in an educational program.

They sound similar, right? There are two small but notable differences. First, unlike standards, competencies can include dispositions—"soft skills"—that generally are overlooked at the standards level (e.g., *thinking flexibly, questioning and posing problems, listening with understanding and empathy,* and all the other Habits of Mind). Second, competencies can be written at the local level, translating the dense language of the standards into phrasing that is accessible for teachers, students, and family members.

So why are competencies gaining traction now? We have our guesses. First, the advent of technology has ushered in the possibility of "anytime, anywhere" learning. If a competency is clear and the instructional and assessment sequence is on a virtual platform, then students can pursue it at their own pace and on their own schedule. Second, key national and state policy and accountability obstacles have been lifted, giving educators a little more breathing room to pursue that which is not required. For example, in the United States, the Every Student Succeeds Act (ESSA) of 2015 allows for greater flexibility to improve schools and scale innovation in relation to personalized learning and competency education by removing structural impediments.

We propose that educators stay committed to a clear, concise, and broad description of our long-term goals: *the desired abilities, skills, and dispositions that our education program is based on.* (Wiggins and McTighe [1998, 2005] refer to these goals as *transfer goals,* the larger aims of a discipline or schooling.) And those long-term goals are these: to have students learn how to pose and pursue rich questions and become adaptive problem-solvers and effective communicators who are both creative and critical in their thinking. In other words, we want students to develop Habits of Mind. The related competencies are the indicators in service of each broader goal.

Figure 3.1, developed with Jay McTighe, highlights both the long-term goals and related competencies of a few disciplines and dispositions.

FIGURE 3.1
Long-Term Goals and Related Competencies

LONG-TERM GOALS	RELATED COMPETENCIES
Career and Technical Education: Develops a career pathway by exploring and pursuing viable options based on interests, talents, and aspirations.	• Sets employment/career goals. • Plans and takes action to gain necessary expertise. • Assembles a résumé/portfolio to demonstrate accomplishment(s).
Physical Education: Plays a chosen game/sport skillfully and with fairness.	• Assesses own performance to set goals to develop/enhance skills. • Conducts self in a sporting manner. • Works toward achievement of group goals (in team sports or group activities).
Math: Addresses complex (messy) problems using mathematical reasoning and perseverance.	• Clarifies the nature of the problem. • Applies appropriate tools/strategies. • Evaluates reasonableness of solution. • Communicates solution/process using mathematical language.
Critical Thinking: Determines whether to accept, reject, or suspend a judgment about a claim.	• Identifies the claim/position. • Asks appropriate clarifying questions. • Judges credibility of a source. • Judges the quality of an argument, including the acceptability of its reasons, assumptions, and evidence. • Draws conclusions when warranted.
Listening with Understanding and Empathy: Devotes mental energy to another's thoughts or ideas. Makes an effort to perceive another's point of view or emotions.	• Paraphrases to affirm understanding. • Demonstrates sensitivity to the feeling and level of knowledge of others. • Asks clarifying questions to understand what the other is saying.

LONG-TERM GOALS	RELATED COMPETENCIES
Creative Thinking: Perceives the world in new ways, finds hidden patterns, makes connections between seemingly unrelated phenomena, and generates new and imaginative solutions.	• Views a situation outside the boundaries of standard conventions. • Generates multiple and alternative statements of a problem. • Connects disparate elements or ideas. • Generates novel/unorthodox solutions or products. • Evaluates possibilities to determine best course of action.
Communication: Conveys information, ideas, and emotions using a variety of media to targeted audiences for a given purpose.	• Expresses ideas clearly. • Communicates appropriately to targeted audience. • Chooses appropriate content, style, and tone suitable to purpose. • Creates quality products in chosen media.
Taking Responsible Risks: Considers risks before taking one. Manages impulsivity yet takes risks when warranted.	• Thinks about new and innovative ideas. • Makes decisions about taking a risk through a thoughtful process. • Shows confidence and is willing to take a chance to further knowing and creating.

Source: Copyright 2017 by Bena Kallick, Allison Zmuda, and Jay McTighe. Used with permission.

Articulating goals and related competencies in this way enables teachers to work together to wrap their arms around the *why*—the broader aims of both the discipline and the dispositions—and how the grade level or course is part of the bigger picture. That is very different from developing goals and competencies focused on grade-level expectations. To break away from a granular frame of reference, where declarative and procedural knowledge is the driving force for what gets taught and tested, teachers need to ensure that students have a broader vision that clarifies the *why* and shows how that broader vision can be broken down into more manageable parts.

Use of SMART Goals to Personalize Literacy

Students also have a role here, and that is understanding what the goals are and planning for how to achieve them. When we spoke to Jessica Craig, a 3rd grade teacher who has been having her students draft SMART goals (strategic/specific, measurable, attainable, realistic/relevant, and time-bound) to personalize literacy time throughout the year, she explained her approach:

> In our class, we use Douglas County School District's World-Class Outcomes. We then took those outcomes and brainstormed smaller areas of focus that would help us reach the larger goal (for example, fluency, accuracy, retell, comprehension, interpretation). Every 6–8 weeks, students choose the area that they feel they need to work on most and collaborate with me to create a SMART goal. They then create a plan to reach that goal and fill their literacy block with activities that will help them grow in that area. It's very important to allow students to share their goal with their families and determine in advance how they will track their progress in order to help them stay accountable.

Figure 3.2 shows a guide for drafting SMART goals that might be distributed to students along with a sample goal.

FIGURE 3.2
A Guide to Drafting Student SMART Goals

SMART GOALS ARE . . .	*MY SMART GOAL*
Strategic & Specific: *What do I want to accomplish?*	I want to improve my speaking and communicating.
Measurable: *How will I know whether or not my goal has been reached?*	I will score myself on a presentation at the end of the month and reflect on how my speaking and communicating have improved.
Attainable: *Is the goal reachable with the resources I have? What are my resources?*	My Personal Learning Activities: 1. Screencasts 2. Independent reading 3. Presentation

SMART GOALS ARE . . .	MY SMART GOAL
Realistic & Relevant: *How does this relate to our past/current unit of inquiries? What's the benefit of reaching this goal?*	These activities will help me improve my literacy and especially my retell. This connects to the "How We Express Ourselves" unit of inquiry that we did earlier this year. I'm learning how to express myself and communicate.
Time-Bound: *When will I meet my goal?*	End of January.

Source: Jessica Craig. Used with permission.

This SMART goal example clarifies how students can learn what the broader goals are in language that is accessible and meaningful to them, work to develop a plan of action and related learning experiences with the teacher, and meaningfully communicate with their families on both their goals and progress. Students own the learning right from the start.

Inquiry/Idea Generation: Finding the Way In

Key Element	Role of the Student and the Teacher	Related Habits of Mind
INQUIRY/IDEA GENERATION *What about the topic sparks your thinking? What is worth pursuing?*	Student independently defines and articulates the problem, idea, design, or investigation. Teacher identifies a broader topic, established inquiry, or problem that can spark student imagination, curiosity, and deeper learning.	• Thinking flexibly • Questioning and problem posing • Creating, imagining, and innovating • Taking responsible risks • Applying past knowledge to new situations • Thinking about your thinking

Learners generate discernable energy when they are immersed in an investigation or deeply engaged in the development of an idea. They engross themselves in figuring out, making sense, creating an idea, testing it out. In these moments, we educators watch them with wonderment and awe, but we also want to work to create the conditions whereby that scenario can happen again and again.

In truth, these periods of energetic inquiry/idea generation are few and far between in most schools. This is partly attributable to how marginalizing the "typical" lesson can seem. Doing what someone else has told you to do feels like a bureaucratic exercise; the student fills out the requisite form to check it off of a "to do" list. The student demonstrates knowledge and skills, and then the experience is over, and the focus changes to some other item on the list—another unmoored task, disconnected from past experiences. There is no room for curiosity. The student becomes more engaged with fulfilling the rules of evaluation and jumping over the predetermined hoops than with the content.

Our task is to move from "learning" that is a series of episodic events to learning that is rich with connection and continuity, and the way forward is by embracing lesson design that features goals linked to inquiry/idea generation. It's about marrying the broader skills and dispositions with a topical exploration. In our view, there are three types of lesson designs that will promote this kind of learning:

1. Ideas or investigations defined by the teacher or the curriculum guide

2. Ideas or investigations co-created with students

3. Independent ideas or investigations in which the student is the primary driver of the experience

Students need consistent experience in all three lesson types— not for every subject and grade level or for every unit or after a certain number of weeks, but often enough for them to feel the occasional misery, frequent messiness, and rewarding magic of developing an investigation or idea. Let's look a little closer at each category.

Ideas or Investigations Defined by the Teacher

This category is grounded in a teacher-generated question, prompt, or challenge within a given unit of study. Students are expected to follow the guidelines or use the scaffolds throughout the learning experience. The following three examples illustrate this approach:

• In a 6th grade mathematics unit, students examine authentic scenarios and consider "what is fair" by applying mean, median, and mode (e.g., how grades are calculated, how U.S. states are represented in Congress, how much money a professional sports athlete is worth to a team). For each example, they need to figure out which measure of central tendency is typically used and whether that is the most reasonable.

• In a yearlong exploration in social studies, 4th graders learn about the geography, economy, and culture of different regions in the United States to make sense of the questions "How would we describe this place? How does it compare to other regions?" The teacher moves students through one region at a time to make those identifications and comparisons.

• In a high school business class, students examine videos of job interviews to consider the question "How do people make a good first impression?" The teacher provides key aspects for students to look for, including how candidates presented their ideas and potential contributions, their responses to questions, their physical appearance, and their speaking manner.

These explorations provide authentic challenges and worthy struggles for students to think their way through, but also enough direction so students don't get lost or wander off on tangents.

Ideas or Investigations Co-Created with Students

This category also relates to a specific curriculum under study. However, in this case, students and teachers partner to determine what is worth investigating or pursuing as an independent venture. As a result, students are more likely to become engaged with deeper learning, as the following examples illustrate:

• In a science unit, 1st graders wonder what makes an object sink or float. The teacher gives them an apple and a pumpkin to test out. Based on their tests, one student suggests that all fruits and vegetables float. A student pulls a banana out of his lunch bag and tests that as well, immediately finding out that the hypothesis is flawed. On the basis of their tests, students try to figure out what makes certain objects sink or float and whether there is a discernable pattern.

• In a middle school unit on natural disasters, students share their experiences about flooding in their community and the damage it caused. As a result of the conversation, one student decides to research and design an emergency preparedness kit tailored for flooding. Another student decides to quantify how much total damage floods cost. A third student decides to capture images of both the devastation and the humanity that come from the tragedy as a reminder of what's most important.

• In a high school U.S. history unit on civil rights, students look at four recent court cases to examine the role of the police and the judicial system in contemporary society, based on their personal experience. The essential questions are "To what extent are the way rules and laws applied to groups of people a form of discrimination? How do we work together to overcome injustice?" Students create their own driving questions to clarify, quantify, and deepen their understanding.

These three classroom examples don't upend the typical organization of school, with its subject-area silos, yet there still is a level of questioning and problem posing, critical thinking, and communication expected in each.

Independent Ideas or Investigations

In this category, students have a deep passion for the pursuit of knowledge because of life circumstances, personal experience, or aspirations, as the following examples show:

• A teenage girl who is going through chemotherapy asks, "When will my hair grow back?" Her mother suggests she pursue her question as her science fair topic. The student does significant research on hair growth for chemotherapy patients, which includes interviewing doctors and fellow cancer survivors, evaluating data contained in scientific journals, and offering a projection based on generalizations gleaned from the data, paired with her unique circumstances.

• Young learners through 12th grade go after a problem or challenge that is weighing heavily on them, such as divorce, bullying, not having enough food to eat, being alone, mental illness, chronic stress, fear of the unknown, fear of the police, and so on. There is a potential for the pursuit to heal—and to offer others comfort, hope, and understanding in similar circumstances.

• A 6th grader wonders about the recent number of teenage concussions in football. He wants to find out more about neuroscience to reevaluate his participation in the sport.

• A 3rd grader is an avid poet and wants to get a volume of her poems published. She examines her private collection to determine which poems are worth sharing and then works to ensure that each poem's message is clear in terms of language, structure, and title.

Alan November (Schwartz, 2014) has described how one of his students who was most resistant to pursuing an independent challenge created a massive database of resources for people with disabilities in her town. November contended, "That's the difference when students define their own problems with intrinsic motivation. They care so much they're begging for the computer lab to stay open during the summer" (para. 15).

The design challenge for the teacher is to make certain the curriculum includes major threads of content that invite investigation, intrigue, a mystery not yet answered. Teachers can structure learning events that invite students to *gather data through all senses*, *respond with wonderment and awe*, and generally make connections that will matter to them, but students also need the opportunity for thought and refinement. The design challenge for students is knowing how to exercise their mental muscles of *questioning and problem posing*; *applying past knowledge to new situations*; *thinking about thinking*; and *creating, imagining, and innovating* in pursuit of the topic or question.

For self-direction to flourish in classrooms, students need guidance from teachers on how to use those mental muscles through a clear introduction to the Habits of Mind, accompanied by a growing development of strategies that help build those habits.

Undesigned Design Time in Manchester Public Schools

We have the good fortune to partner with Connecticut's Manchester Public Schools around personalized learning with Habits of Mind. The district is currently playing with what it calls *undesigned design time*, and part of that work is to promote student-driven projects at the high school level.

A one-credit pilot seminar was offered in which students could design a project with teacher support. Approximately 60 students and 30 teachers volunteered to venture into the unknown in spite of—or excited by—the fact that there were no existing lesson plans, no allotted class meeting times, and no established grading and reporting policies. Figure 3.3 shows what students and teachers hoped to get out of the opportunity.

Students and teachers gathered together with one of us to facilitate this new venture. At the beginning of the session, teachers were a bit nervous about whether it would work—it *was* uncharted territory. Because it was their inclination to advise the students, they had *to manage their impulsivity* and start by *listening with understanding and empathy* before giving any advice. The risk for teachers was to allow students to lead the inquiry/idea generation without giving them any specific directions. The shift, for teachers, was to be the listeners and, for students, to be the storytellers.

The students were also nervous. Their risk was to describe a dream or aspiration in a stage of incubation. One student wanted to complete a novel she started a few years ago. Another wanted to design stilts for a circus act. Students noted some of the roadblocks they had run up against in previous projects: not being able to stick with it, working in a group in which some of the members didn't participate, losing inspiration, balancing time, and changing their minds about what they wanted to do midstream.

FIGURE 3.3
Undesigned Design Time: Student and Teacher Expectations

STUDENT EXPECTATIONS	TEACHER EXPECTATIONS
• To explore and share ideas in ways that I don't usually get to in the classroom. • To get more comfortable communicating with others. • To study and learn about what I want to rather than what others say I should. • To have one-on-one experiences with my teacher. • To discover new ideas, hobbies, and things that interest me. • To figure out new ways to help people and connect with them. • To try out something I like. • To get hands-on experience in a profession, which may help me figure out what I want to do.	• To work with students with diverse ideas, function as a sounding board, and help them to move forward. • To create a more personal connection with students. • To gain ideas for experiences that could be transferred into the classroom and used to develop greater student engagement. • To step back from completely directing and structuring students' learning experiences and take on a consultative role as they design and redesign their own paths. • To explore ways to connect with students outside a teacher's traditional "knowledge keeper" role.

We then asked, "What does it mean when you say someone has an attitude?" Students described both positive and negative attitudes, as well as the role of body language. We then introduced the Habits of Mind, the idea that these "attitudes" can become habits that the students can control. When they *create, imagine, and innovate* or *apply past knowledge to new situations*, for example, they convey something about themselves as learners, which shows in their body language, in the ways they interact with one another, and in how they interact with the world beyond school.

Next, we shifted our focus to practice *listening with understanding and empathy*. In groups of three (two students, one staff mentor), each student had to respond aloud to the prompt "As I consider a project, I am thinking . . ." while the mentor and other student listened. When we debriefed how it felt to be listened to so closely, student comments testified to the power of this new territory:

• "It felt weird. I'm not used to doing that much talking about my ideas."

- "Most of the time in school, I feel like teachers don't really know anything about me. I'm just another student. I don't think teachers think we have ideas. I felt that the teacher really listened to me and to my ideas."

- "I found myself choosing my words very carefully. I wanted to make sure I was understood."

- "I found that I was giving more detail about what I was saying. I was ready to stop at a more superficial level, but then I needed to think more about what I was saying."

- "I go home [after school] and don't talk to anyone. I go up to my room and text. I don't have anyone who listens to me. I'm quiet in school. This was a very different experience for me."

In these words, we begin to see the shifting roles of teacher and student, the early signs of new partnership, and how "weird" it may feel initially for all involved.

Good Questions at Aveson Charter School

There is a different energy to this work, one in which the student has an increased level of ownership in both the inquiry and pursuit. At Aveson Charter Schools in Altadena, California, student-driven learning experiences are integral. Figure 3.4 shows a rubric Aveson created that is focused on developing complex questions.

FIGURE 3.4
Rubric on Levels of Questioning

1—EMERGING	2—DEVELOPING	3—PROFICIENT	4—ADVANCED
I can create a question.	With much support, I can create a science- or history-related question.	I can create an open-ended question related to science or history with little support.	I can independently create an open-ended question that is provocative (exciting) and can arise in the real world.

1—EMERGING	2—DEVELOPING	3—PROFICIENT	4—ADVANCED
My Driving Question has a framing word.	My Driving Question has a framing word and a challenge.	My Driving Question has a framing word, an entity/person, and a challenge.	My Driving Question has a framing word, an entity/person, a challenge, and an audience/purpose.
My Driving Question raises science- or history-related issues with a predetermined answer.	I need help to determine which type of question it is: philosophical/debatable, task/role-oriented, or evaluative/quantitative-oriented.	I can determine which type of question it is: philosophical/debatable, task/role-oriented, or evaluative/quantitative-oriented.	I can independently determine which type of question it is: philosophical/debatable, task/role-oriented, or evaluative/quantitative-oriented.

Source: Aveson Charter School, Altadena, CA. Used with permission.

Teacher-advisors offer the sentence frames shown in Figure 3.5 to provide instructional support, communicate feedback, and collaborate with students to craft the action steps that will further investigation.

FIGURE 3.5
Sentence Frames for Three Kinds of Questions

Evaluative or Quantitative (Proving) Questions

Ask these questions when you are trying to prove or defend something by evaluating or analyzing information or data.

- What makes a good _____?
- What are the ingredients for a successful _____?
- What is the best way to _____?
- Does _____ affect _____?
- What are the advantages and disadvantages of _____?
- What will happen if _____?
- How many different _____ are there?
- In what ways did _____ influence _____?

Continued

FIGURE 3.5 (CONTINUED)
Sentence Frames for Three Kinds of Questions

Philosophical or Debatable (Knowing) Questions

Ask these questions when you are trying to apply facts to address complexity.

- Is _____ really important? Why?
- What would _____ be without _____?
- Did _____ influence _____?
- How are _____ and _____ different?
- Is there a relationship between _____ and _____?

Role-Oriented or Plan of Action (Doing) Questions

Ask these questions when you are taking on a role to solve a problem or conflict or trying to complete a project.

- What would I, in the role of a _____, need to do to achieve the outcome I want?
- If I do _____, what is the next action I would need to take? Would I also need to _____?
- What consequences might come from doing _____? Would it change the outcome of _____?

Source: Aveson Charter Schools, Altadena, CA. Used with permission.

Recommendations and Concerns

To close this chapter, we offer a handful of common "yes, buts" we have heard in our work with teachers who want to figure out personalized learning and are committed to doing what is best for kids, but who are, at the same time, understandably cautious about making a leap that will unravel a good many instructional habits and routines.

Yes, but... how do you structure personalized learning? One way to engage in this type of exploration is by offering the *genius hour*—typically, one period a week in which students can pursue any idea or become more expert at something. Students use this time to develop, reflect, and seek out feedback and guidance. In most cases, students present the results of their pursuits toward the end of the year. They reflect on what they have chosen, why it is important, and how and to whom it matters. Genius hour events usually focus more on developing dispositions than on evaluating the overall result. Students develop strategies for *persisting* when faced with uncertainty, *taking responsible risks* as they play with new ideas, and share in the excitement as they observe their work with *wonderment and awe.*

A second and more formal example is a culminating project or capstone experience, in which students pursue an area of interest at the end of a year or end of a school experience just before transitioning (e.g., in 8th or 12th grade). Each student develops an idea to demonstrate skills and dispositions within and across subject areas. These "capstones" typically are anchored in pursuit of a question and result in a formal presentation, performance, or project. The power of these opportunities resides in the fact that students come to see them as "what we do at school," rather than as a specialized experience. They also offer an important context for practicing Habits of Mind because students are required to describe why their topic is important, why it matters, and how they might transfer the habits they're practicing to other learning experiences.

Yes, but... how do you teach them to do personalized learning? Terry Heick (2013) created a fabulous guide for teachers on the four phases of inquiry-based learning, which is very much in line with the inquiry/idea generation we describe here. We present a condensed version of this guide in Figure 3.6. (see p. 48). To see the full guide, go to www.teachthought.com/pedagogy/4-phases -inquiry-based-learning-guide-teachers.

Yes, but... how do you have time for personalized learning and time to teach what you're supposed to? Many teachers start small to test time management. For example, one high school teacher we know decided to make every Friday a project-based learning day. He designed his curriculum to include the opportunity for students to use the media lab on Friday as a place of further investigation. Gradually, the students became so intrigued with their projects that he found ways to reorganize the time in his classroom. The more rigid agenda eventually gave way to a more flexible arrangement of blended learning and media center use.

Finding the time does not mean that there will be more time "found." It means changing how both you and your students use time. This is where technology plays a significant role. Teachers can

FIGURE 3.6
Heick's 4 Phases of Inquiry-Based Learning

1. Interaction. Student wants to figure out or make sense of something (by way of materials, peers, experts, media) and is not burdened by strict parameters or a time line.

Student Indicators: Actively skims a variety of media, follows curiosity, responds with awe, dwells with certain media depending on curiosity or perceived utility; seeks out peers for ideas and resources.

Teacher Indicators: Models curiosity, thinks aloud when interacting with disparate media, asks probing questions, withholds evaluative statements, provides exemplars, monitors and encourages student thinking habits.

2. Clarification. Student analyzes information to determine patterns and identify misconceptions; "gets a feel" for the scale, nature, and possibility of selected topics of inquiry to clarify own thinking.

Student Indicators: Paraphrases understanding in familiar language; resists looking for answers and solutions; distinguishes between fact and opinion; evaluates the credibility and relevance of sources; focuses on possibility.

Teacher Indicators: Offers nonevaluative and frequent feedback; provides relevant graphic organizers and other ways to frame student thinking; asks probing questions that focus on student thinking—what they know, and why they think they know it.

3. Questioning. Student focuses on deepening knowledge base and understanding, which requires continued questioning and problem posing, perseverance, and thinking flexibly.

Student Indicators: Is curious, precise with questions, self-monitoring; engages in big-picture thinking and little-picture application.

Teacher Indicators: Models questioning, thinks aloud in revising irrelevant or otherwise flawed questions; models use of concept-mapping tools to analyze thinking; hosts question formulation technique (QFT) sessions and Socratic seminars.

4. Design. Student shares results of research with target audience based on his or her problem, idea, or topic.

Student Indicators: Clarifies thinking, is self-directed, is uncertain but efficacious, follows curiosity.

Teacher Indicators: Creates conditions and means for collaboration; identifies areas for revision; reflects on entire process (that is, *How did we get to this point?*)

Source: From *4 Phases of Inquiry-Based Learning: A Guide for Teachers,* by T. Heick, 2013, TeachThought. Copyright 2016 by TeachThought. Adapted with permission.

create "playlists" that students can use to cover key points in the curriculum at their own pace. Classroom spaces can be designed with specific kinds of learning in mind—for example, with a seminar space, where teachers can come together with small groups of students for in-depth instructional time; with a work space, where students can develop prototypes and models for their investigations; and with a "cave," where students can be alone for focused and quiet attention. Naming the spaces names the intention and is a reminder of the behaviors expected in those spaces. In the course of this implementation, students develop effective management plans and find the time they need to do the work.

To Sum Up

Students greatly benefit when they engage in personalized learning experiences. They are eager to commit to authentic learning that they have participated in co-creating. They have a real curiosity about the way the world operates and, when given the opportunity, will dive deeply to answer their questions.

Students are growing up in a world that is eminently accessible to them through technology. This gives us an opportunity to provide them with an education that reaches for long-term life goals as well as short-term, in-the-moment goals. As we move toward better defining the competencies associated with these broader, long-term goals, students will become better at telling us what they know and how they know it. Ultimately, it will be up to us, the adults in their world, to be good listeners as we encourage them to ask the questions and create new knowledge.

How Students Can Show
What They Know

*Task and Audience, Evaluation, and Cumulative
Demonstration of Learning*

When students are invited to the design table and become invested in their own designs, they are more likely to embark on an experience of deep learning. Classroom boundaries seem to disappear as the learner becomes attuned to the intrigue of the investigation, to the practice necessary to develop a precise skill, to what can be imagined and made.

All this is possible when teachers ease off the familiar curriculum and assessment sprint and embrace students as partners. If our long-term goals are to create self-directed and "thought-full" problem solvers, critical and creative thinkers, and compassionate listeners, then the way we develop instruction to build and assess those competencies has to be more open to student *voice, co-creation, social construction*, and *self-discovery*.

In this chapter, we explore the key concerns for teachers and students when designing personalized learning with the end in mind. They are **task and audience**—how students will define the task and determine the most appropriate audience; **evaluation**—how the work will be judged, including the critical consideration of self-evaluation; and **cumulative demonstration of learning**—how students will review and demonstrate their cumulative work over time, discovering more about who they are as learners and what interests them most.

Task and Audience: Providing Students a Seat at the Design Table

Key Element	Role of the Student and the Teacher	Related Habits of Mind
TASK AND AUDIENCE *How does audience shape creation and communication?*	Student identifies and engages with an authentic audience to help create, test, and refine the task. Teacher helps to establish an appropriate audience for the task and guides the student toward a performance forum in which the work will have an impact.	• Listening with understanding and empathy • Striving for accuracy • Communicating with clarity and precision • Thinking interdependently • Thinking about your thinking • Taking responsible risks

There are three design and performance opportunities for students and teachers to consider in relation to **task and audience**: *student as participant, student as co-creator,* and *student as driver.* As illustrated in Figure 4.1 (see p. 52), the three roles overlap, and students can shift among them depending on personal needs, time parameters, and goals. Each approach has its advantages but also carries some cautions to bear in mind.

Student as participant. Students have the opportunity to choose from a set of teacher-approved topics, texts, or challenges. For example, they might

- Select one topic to research from a list of topics.
- Read one of several given texts on a chosen theme.
- Select one of several objects to reimagine.
- Make a persuasive case for or against a controversial issue.

The advantages: The teacher can tailor the task more directly to a particular unit or to grade-level expectations and honor the range of student interests in the classroom. Students can exercise choice and still feel as though they have enough structure to avoid getting lost.

FIGURE 4.1
Student Design and Performance Opportunities

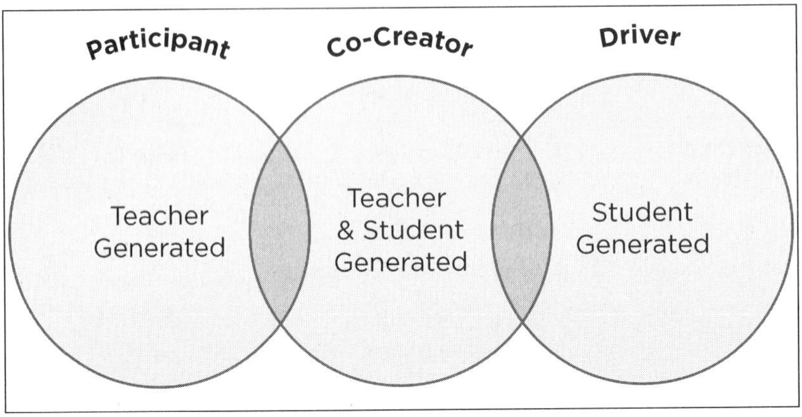

The cautions: The teacher has a lot of heavy design lifting to do. Creating even a handful of options requires time to find and pursue ideas that are relevant to the content and meaningful to students. And just because the teacher has offered two or three choices, it doesn't mean that every student has a choice that is a good fit.

Student as co-creator. Students have the opportunity to steer task design within a given set of teacher-developed parameters. They might

• Write in a given genre to demonstrate understanding of that genre.

• Investigate a local, national, or global problem, such as inequality in the distribution of income in the United States.

• Develop a travel itinerary based on exploration of cultures.

The advantages: Sharing task-design responsibilities allows the teacher to focus on the broader problem, design challenge, idea, or genre that pays attention to both the content of the curriculum and, at the same time, to the talents and interests of the students. Within broad, agreed-to task guidelines, students can pursue whatever aspect of the lesson content they find most relevant, important, and meaningful.

The cautions: The teacher has to consult with students one on one to develop a coordinated plan and timelines for various task stages, monitor progress, and offer appropriate support. Students may get a bit lost and look to the teacher for ideas—at which time their role starts to shift toward student as participant (see Figure 4.1). In addition, within one classroom there is likely to be a wide range of co-created tasks, leaving students without a direct peer model to inspire their work.

Student as driver. Here, students embark on a task of their own design guided only by evaluation criteria—either externally developed (from an organization or from competition or industry specifications) or internally developed (from school requirements or teacher expectations). For example, they might

- Conduct and document an experiment for the science fair.
- Engage in a regular genius hour exploration throughout the year where students can pursue *any* idea through research, create a text, or take action in the community.
- Complete a capstone experience at the end of 5th, 8th, or 12th grade.
- Write a short story for a writing competition.
- Prepare an original monologue for an open mike session.

The advantages: The teacher leverages criteria to encourage student exploration, deep thinking, and creation. Students can pursue challenges and create ideas that matter to them. They work to satisfy the established criteria, but they are also driven by their own aspiration to produce what they see as quality work.

The cautions: The teacher *must* find time for one-on-one conferences scheduled to reflect student needs related to goal setting, monitoring, and deadlines. Frequent check-ins may be absolutely necessary for one student yet stifling for another. Some students may become unmoored, especially if this type of experience is foreign to them. They may be so used to operating with clear teacher direction that this opportunity feels more like paralysis than liberation.

New Responsibilities in a New Kind of Relationship

In all three design and performance opportunities, the students' place at the design table demonstrates respect for them as learners. However, teachers and students will need to feel their way through this new collaborative relationship. Teachers will need to build relationships with students based on knowing their strengths and talents. They will have to resist overwhelming the students' participation with personal experiences and agendas. They must be prepared for far more give and take as opposed to having the classroom organized exclusively around the teacher's authority.

Students, now invited to interact with the curriculum rather than regard it as a fixed agenda, need to learn how to articulate their interests and the questions they have as they go about choosing areas they want to purposefully pursue. They are now expected to engage in discussions of what really matters for a given product or performance. Although conversation might start with their individual perspective on what quality looks like, it must grow through collective examination and discussion into a sense of what quality looks like across a range of products or performances for a given genre (e.g., a scientific journal, a one-act play, a persuasive speech).

As the students become co-creators of the design challenge of their choice, they work with teachers and peers to determine their course of action—what their approach will be and how they will consider presenting their work to an audience. From the outset of every task, it is important for students to *think about their thinking*—considering their work habits, reflecting on their capacity to *persist*, and remembering the strategies that have worked for them in the past. This examination and articulation can help students break down the walls that separate "school work" and "real work," making the assignment more relevant.

Getting Inspired as You Co-Create

When designing performance opportunities, the first order of business is to contemplate *purpose, audience,* and *task*. Any one of the three can be the entry point, but all three must be thought through and aligned with one another. For example, you may be hunting around online for new ways to inspire students to demonstrate their learning and come across something like the word cloud in Figure 4.2.

FIGURE 4.2
A Collection of Performance Possibilities

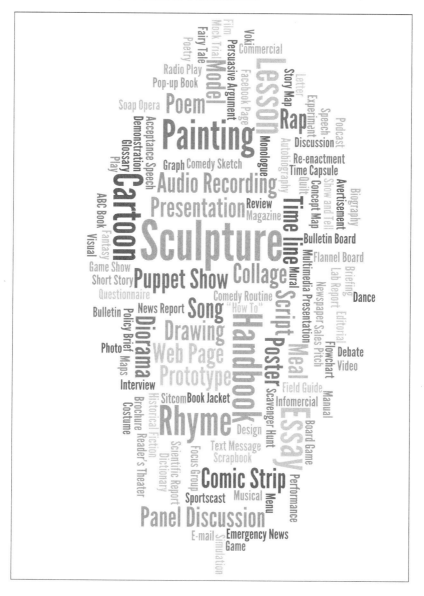

Lists such as this illustrate the opportunity and the challenge. Any of the suggested ways "to show what you know" can either feel gimmicky or authentic, depending on its connection to the topic and how well the person carrying out that task understands effective communication within the specified form.

For example, from a student's point of view, doing a news report can be a fantastic opportunity, provided that the student knows how to select and investigate a worthy problem or challenge; make sense of differing viewpoints to ensure the report is well researched, trustworthy, and balanced; and share the report in a way that will resonate with the target audience. Compare that experience with that of a student who is assigned a topic, finds information and takes notes, and presents findings using the form of a written newspaper report or a recorded or live event with the teacher serving as the sole audience. The latter amounts to a "bad karaoke" version of the former's powerful learning.

Here are some additional examples of how ways to "show what you know" can grow into rewarding and engaging co-created tasks:

• *Comedy routines.* This presentation format allows students to demonstrate how humor can be used to tackle serious issues, such as race relations, illegal immigration, and obesity. (Note that students will need to understand what makes a joke funny, how to use jokes to address complex social issues, and how to get the right blend of seriousness and levity.) Students can produce a comedy routine or analyze how a professional comedian might navigate this territory. This can be an excellent way to deepen their understanding of the habit of *finding humor.*

• *Original videos and comics.* Both formats provide students with ways to demonstrate their grasp of content topics and teach this content to others. As middle school math teacher Eric Marcos has done, a teacher can create a virtual space with a global audience in which students can create and share math tutorials (see http://mathtrain.tv/category/student-created-videos). Many of the tutorials Eric's students created have been viewed thousands of times by viewers who not only benefit from the content but also provide a rating on how helpful it was. For an example of how content understanding can be conveyed through comics created with software tools such as Comic Life, ShowMe, and Educreations, check out student work samples collected by technology specialist and blogger John Stevens at www.fishing 4tech.com/student-work-samples.html.

• *Time capsules.* As a performance opportunity, curating the contents of a time capsule gives students a way to illustrate their understanding of historical and contemporary issues, values, and innovations through the artifacts they identify and the rationale they offer for the inclusion of each. A time capsule can be physical (housed in a container) or virtual (a collection of media artifacts, such as short looping videos and infographics).

• *Virtual book discussions.* When conducted through platforms such Global Read Aloud (https://theglobalreadaloud.com), virtual book discussions allow students to join age-level discussions with peers who bring a wide range of perspectives to different texts. A reflection prompt can ask students to consider how this global conversation affected their understanding of the text. Since 2010, more than 500,000 connections have been made through discussions within and across classrooms through tools such as Twitter, Kidblog, and Edmodo.

• *How-to demonstrations.* Whether recorded or not, how-to demonstrations—such as "How to Make Compost," "How to Build an Insect Hotel," and "How to Conduct a Taste Test"—can provide students opportunities to share their mastery of real-world skills and procedural knowledge and teach it to others. The examples mentioned are just some of the ways students have illustrated mastery of curriculum of Alice Waters's The Edible Schoolyard (www .edibleschoolyard.org), which is aligned with the Common Core and the Next Generation Science Standards.

• *Fan fiction.* The creative writing exercise of reimagining an author's published work with new beginnings, endings, and scenes has been used in classrooms for decades. With the advent of virtual publishing has come an explosion of fan fiction, or fanfic—millions of written works that embellish, alter, or expand copyrighted works in a range of genres, including film and television scripts. Fanfic can feature new story lines, characters, beginnings, or endings, and might substitute sets of morals, ideals, or political viewpoints. Students can demonstrate their ability to use narrative techniques to develop experiences and events or show the responses of characters to situations. They might provide a story line or ending that follows from narrated experiences or events (adapted from the Common Core English Language Arts standards) and post their work on websites like www.fanfiction.net (which stipulates a minimum contributor age of 13 years old) or participate in competitions. For example, Metro Library in Oklahoma City, Oklahoma, has an annual competition open to all ages. For more information on creating fan fiction, check out www.wikihow.com/Write-a-Fanfiction.

• *Pitching design ideas.* This performance option allows students to apply content understanding to real-world problems or make everyday life easier. On Design Squad Global (http://pbskids.org/designsquad/projects), young students imagine, share, and build on ideas on the site. Students have designed a fan with a built-in smoke alarm and fire extinguisher, a video game for the blind, and a robot that can search for missing people.

The Power of Authentic Audience

Craig Gastauer, a high school science teacher in California, has experienced firsthand the difference authentic audiences can make. Here's how he described it to us:

> Most of the students in my course (52 of 56 students) believed that focusing on a specific audience changed how they approached their learning. Many students noted that perspective mattered. Although two different audiences may want to know how to help a dehydrated child, a rescue worker may want to hear scientifically worded instructions, whereas the parents may not. Still other students realized that their method of communication required more than just skill in the use of grammar and punctuation. They had to organize their learning and produce coherent thoughts because their final

product was going to be presented to an authentic audience. This placed more pressure on them to demonstrate that they had learned and could transfer their knowledge.

Unfortunately, the open-ended nature of the task, audience, and format did create anxiety. One student wrote, "For years we are taught that following rules and the given format is the only way to be successful. Now we are being told to step out of the box. I was a little lost on how to begin. However, this method allows me to explore my options and decide on what is the best possible way to present what I know."

Other students focused on the fear of getting a bad grade or fear of responsibility. Here are some of their comments:

- "I think the teacher should tell and show the students exactly how to do the work so there is no question. I'll get a good grade that way."
- "I like defined structure. If the teacher told me what to do, I would feel more confident in what I produce."
- "Indecisiveness plays a large role in my world."
- "All my other teachers tell me what to do and how to do it. Why should I be made uncomfortable in this class?"

But one student's insight made it clear that this work is worth doing: "If the teacher ends up telling you how to do everything, you will never really understand why or what you're doing because the teacher does most of the thinking and work for you."

I am more committed than ever to co-create opportunities for students to engage in organizing knowledge and processes, to critically think and make sense of their learning, and to transfer their understanding to novel situations to prepare them for their future.

Offer Exemplars, Seek Expertise

It's important to provide exemplars for students as they engage in their learning tasks so they can consider what they are investigating and for what purpose. Often this is an iterative process; students may delve into an investigation with one product in mind and then realize that the chosen task does not translate well to the intended audience. For example, if they want to show opposite perspectives, a debate may be the first choice. However, after investigation, they may decide that although the opposite perspectives are important, their real intention is to advocate for one of those perspectives. Therefore, they may choose to create an informational website that fosters advocacy and problem solving. They realize that their purpose is to inform the public, and that this is best served over the Internet. They might contact a person who designs websites or a nonprofit organization that uses its own website for the same purpose.

Notice, also, the interdisciplinary nature of this sort of development. Perhaps the art teacher can contribute to an understanding of aesthetic presentation, the physical education teacher can become the content expert because the project is about a health issue, or the English teacher can offer expertise on how to craft persuasive text. The expertise is both within and outside the school.

Recommendations to Turn Students into Co-Creators

Remember that "compelling" has a current twist. Learners want to make sense of how curriculum content relates to their current circumstances, challenges, or worldview. Work that involves doing a deep dive into the past, for example, needs to be grounded in something that matters to the learner, to his or her community, or to the world *today*. The design challenge is to frame the problem and include students early on in curriculum development so that you can see what is compelling to both individual students and to the class as a whole.

Focus on the end goal, and let go of some of the control. Staying focused on the purpose—on what you are trying to accomplish in service of learning—can ease students' transition to the co-creator role and your transition, too. The idea of having lots of tasks happening all at once is overwhelming to many teachers. But remember, we are not just throwing students into the deep end and wishing them good luck, and we are not enabling them to do whatever they want irrespective of the subject-area requirements. What we are doing is inviting students into a process—into a balancing act in which we help them think through what questions to pose, what to create, for whom to create it, and how to *communicate about it with clarity and precision*.

Remember that authenticity matters. Authentic problems, issues, and ideas that students generate and pursue require investigation and deep thinking. Such ideas live in the world of citizens, experts, and visionaries. Authentic audiences can offer feedback and guidance to help refine a student's idea, solution, or understanding of the problem.

Remember that practice matters. Having students focus on becoming a better scientist, historian, artist, mathematician, or chef requires regular opportunities to engage in authentic work. Gillian Epstein, a writing consultant and professor at Olin College in Massachusetts, works with engineering students on their capacity to offer insight into their own lives through their writing.

Epstein shared with us two key pieces of advice for growing student writers. The first is that teachers should ask students to tell "small" stories from their lives (small, as in requiring no more than one single-spaced page). She noted that this "frees them up to put anything on the table without self-censorship, avoids the paralysis of writer's block, and makes rewriting feel accessible instead of onerous." Second, teachers should consider having students solicit and share stories beyond the classroom. For example, they might interview an elderly community member to hear a new take on issues that might have surfaced in their own lives—things like challenging authority, grieving a loss, making a mistake, or compromising a dream. This approach not only broadens the students' perspective but also connects them to traditions of storytelling, questioning, and sharing that bring in discoveries from the world and bring a classroom to life.

Evaluation: Providing Students a Place at the Judging Table

Key Element	Role of the Student and the Teacher	Related Habits of Mind
EVALUATION *How is performance evaluated on a given task using criteria?*	Student collaboratively defines evaluative criteria or works within existing criteria to self-evaluate while developing a product/performance. Teacher collaboratively defines or reviews criteria with student(s) to facilitate ongoing evaluation of a product/performance.	• Striving for accuracy • Remaining open to continuous learning • Gathering data from all senses • Thinking about your thinking • Responding with wonderment and awe

In order for students to settle into the design and development of a given task, they also need to know how they will be measured. Delineating criteria and related scoring tools clarifies and supports student development.

Co-Creating the Rubric

Many teachers have experienced the arduous and meticulous process of drafting a rubric using a cycle of design, testing, and feedback-based refinement. We are suggesting that students participate in this process. When students enter the science fair, for example, they pursue something they wonder about through investigational design. They select the topic, question, hypothesis, and approach; consulting with experts, they develop the evaluative criteria that will guide their work. Having an external audience for these projects is, of course, important, as is the fact that students must be able to communicate the relevance of the study—why it's important and why it matters *to them.*

We will look at this process of co-creating the rubric through three lenses: quality of the performance or product, authorship of the rubric, and ownership of the result.

Quality of the performance or product. To what extent did the performance or product convey the message for the desired purpose and audience? To what extent was the designed solution innovative? To what extent did it solve the problem? To what extent was the claim successfully justified or refuted?

These statements hearken back to our broader goals of focusing on the process, as well as evaluating the finished result. Evaluating the performance goes beyond students rating themselves on a scoring checklist or rubric for the teacher to consider before entering a grade. **Evaluation** requires rich feedback from the student, which can be elicited through reflective prompts the student responds to, either in writing or as part of a conference.

Quality now becomes more than something defined solely by the teacher; students have their own set of standards they want to meet. When the work is a reflection of their deeper thinking, students care more about the details, nuances, and techniques than with a stand-alone assignment. Students step back and take a look at the product or performance: *Was it an elegant solution? Did what I create mean something to me? Did it mean something to others?*

Students also need to recognize the growth of knowledge and skill sets: *What do I know now about the topic, question, or problem that I could not have imagined a few weeks or months ago? How did focusing on and practicing specific techniques or procedures affect the overall result?*

Finally, students need to celebrate both the process and performance: *How did I overcome challenges?* Documenting these reflections to accompany the performance solidifies the accomplishment. What students did and how they did it is a testament to what they are capable of if they work hard, grow from feedback, and trust their vision.

Authorship of the rubric. Teachers spend a considerable amount of time designing rubrics, checklists, and other methods for students to learn the criteria and standards by which they will be evaluated. However, our ultimate goal is for students to become self-evaluating. Our purpose is for them to see the *external* criteria that are designed for scoring as well as recognize their own *internal* standards and criteria that describe the level and kind of work they want to produce.

In many instances, the internal and external criteria are the same. However, sometimes students believe that some of the criteria don't match their perception about what really matters in their work. For example, they may feel that the most significant aspect of their work is the incorporation of graphic design—visual elements that stand in for written text—and object to this element not being "covered" in the rubric. They may disagree with the limitations of the standards statements. They may feel that the rubric forced them in a direction that they did not want to go, but they realized that their grade depended on following the rubric. For all these reasons, co-creating the rubric can facilitate ownership of the design criteria.

There are several important considerations when opening up authorship to students. First, developing quality rubrics is a meticulous endeavor that requires significant attention to detail. Students who are engaging in this, especially for the first few times, need to understand what it requires of them so they don't give up, clam up, or become satisfied with someone taking over the process. Second, developing quality rubrics has to be done in conjunction with broader goals—demonstration of concepts, skills, and dispositions aligned with related standards. For many students, the rubric statements may be difficult to grasp because of their sophisticated vocabulary and dense text. It's helpful to work through and reframe everything in language that is accessible to students so they can be partners in articulating and verifying alignment. Third, there has to be enough space to co-create and test out rubrics to ensure they appropriately guide student development. Fourth, when students create rubrics at the classroom level, they may become more critical of rubrics that are set by a subject area or used schoolwide.

Ownership of the result. Whether students play a significant role in the development of the rubrics or not, every student deserves to examine a rubric in relation to the work of others (students, professionals in the field) to open up their minds to possibilities as well as identify quality models to inspire their own work. As students examine work in relation to established criteria, they become more aware of what constitutes quality. These experiences motivate students to make their work the best it can be, resulting in a growing sense of pride in what they create and do. Having a range of concrete examples anchors the rubric, offering a touchstone that students can revisit periodically when they need inspiration.

Recommendations to Make Evaluation a Joint Endeavor

Make the scoring tool a trusted friend. Whether you are using a traditional rubric or badges on a competency continuum, try to keep the tool as stable as possible for the genre of performance. Speaking, problem solving, design, and informative writing can all be well described and repurposed for the topic at hand.

For example, Avon Public Schools in Connecticut drafted districtwide rubrics for literacy learning tailored to literary analysis, informational text, argumentation, and presentational modes. During the first year of implementation, the teachers further evaluated the rubrics and personalized them to align with individual performance tasks. In addition to being a communication tool for students, the new rubrics have proven valuable to parents, teachers, and administrators. Figure 4.3 (see p. 66) shows a kindergarten rubric for informational text that teachers include on the reverse side of a piece of student writing. It connects student work with the Common Core standards and the district curriculum and provides valuable information to parents.

Mark it up, make it better. Rubrics should be written on and owned by the student, regardless of original authorship. Encourage students to highlight unfamiliar words and underline key phrases to clarify areas of confusion, as well as identify areas of priority or significance. Part of the markup process may reveal more concise, clearer, or more meaningful language for students, which teachers might use to refine the rubric and make it more student-friendly.

FIGURE 4.3
Kindergarten Rubric for Informational Texts

Informative Rubric Aligned with ELA Standards, Grade K

Standards Aligned to Ideas and Content

CCSS.ELA-LITERACY.W.K.2. Use a combination of drawing, dictating, and writing to compose informative/explanatory texts in which they name what they are writing about and supply some information about the topic.

Criteria	1 – Beginning	2 – Developing	3 – Proficient	4 – Advanced
Ideas and Content *Is my message clear, detailed, and on topic?*	My writing does not have a topic OR my details are inaccurate or are not related to my topic *I love mom.*	My writing has a topic, but I do not give information about the topic. *Birds. I like birds. Birds are cool.*	My writing has a topic and at least one accurate detail that describes or explains it. *Birds can fly. Birds have feathers.*	My writing clearly states a topic and has relevant and specific details to describe and explain it. *Birds can lay eggs. Some birds have red feathers. Birds fly.*

CCSS.ELA-LITERACY.W.K.5. With guidance and support from adults, respond to questions and suggestions from peers and add details to strengthen writing as needed.

CCSS.ELA-LITERACY.L.K.1.B. Use frequently occurring nouns and verbs.

Criteria	1 – Beginning	2 – Developing	3 – Proficient	4 – Advanced
Word Choice *Do I think about the words I choose?*	My words do not give information or describe the topic.	I start to use words/ vocabulary that give information and describe the topic.	I use specific words/ vocabulary that give accurate information and describe the topic.	I consistently use specific words/vocabulary that give accurate information and clearly describe the topic.

Source: Avon Public Schools, Avon, CT. Used with permission.

Students might indicate areas of measurement they believe should be added to the rubric or signal areas that might not apply to some or all of students' products or performances.

Rewind to the beginning. Have students take a look at their initial renderings, strategies, questions, and knowledge base. For example, we hear students say, "You know, when I got the feedback in our critical friends group, I was able to make changes I didn't realize were really needed" or, "In the beginning, I could not figure out what I really wanted to do, but as I look back on the progress I've made, I see that the turning point came when I visited with someone over a Skype call."

Of course, this kind of reflection is strengthened when students are required to document the various stages of their product from start to finish. Voice recordings, snapshots of work, graphic organizers, and free writes are just a handful of ways for students to capture their work throughout its development so that they can more effectively reflect on it at its conclusion.

Change who the power broker is. We want students to let go of the idea that grading is something that's "done to them" and learn how to critique their own work. Critically, we want them to see this opportunity not as a novelty but as an extension of what it means to be a true learning partner. We care that students develop the capacity to evaluate their depth of content knowledge, skill development, conceptual understanding, and overall satisfaction within and beyond their school performances.

Practice passing judgment. Students should become increasingly comfortable with the scoring tool through the process of evaluating others' work and identifying strengths and possible areas of improvement. Regular experience in the evaluation role provides students with the opportunity to see a current performance in context. It underscores the essential lesson that there is always room for improvement that is based on clear and actionable feedback.

Cumulative Demonstration of Learning: Generating a Truer Picture of Growth

Key Element	Role of the Student and the Teacher	Related Habits of Mind
CUMULATIVE DEMONSTRATION OF LEARNING *How do we show evidence of learning over time?*	Student shapes a representative body of work accomplished over time in a portfolio or exhibition that demonstrates disciplinary, cross-disciplinary, and dispositional competencies. Student recognizes the strengths and weaknesses of this work and sets future directions for learning. Teacher confers with student, acting as a sounding board, and helps to qualify the credibility of the evidence of learning, based on a close reading of the outcomes. Teacher recognizes specific strengths and weaknesses of the work and celebrates the success and achievements of the student.	• Applying past knowledge to new situations • Remaining open to continuous learning • Communicating with clarity and precision • Responding with wonderment and awe

This final section of the chapter describes a more holistic view of growth over time through **cumulative demonstration of learning**, which typically involves portfolios or exhibitions. Our internal compass, our capacity to listen to others and learn from short-term results, and our collective vision and direction help the entire school community reimagine an architecture that is good for both children and adults. We can focus on the end in mind *and* track progress toward that destination. We can improve quality on specific personalized tasks *and* engage in self-discovery along the way. We can evaluate student achievement *and* encourage students to set their own high expectations that may endure long after the assignment is over.

We endorse a "body of evidence of achievement and growth," as suggested by Jay McTighe and Grant Wiggins (2011):

> Like a photo album, it provides a more complete and accurate portrayal of a learner than does any single test score ("snapshot"). It enables "triangulation" of data from multiple sources, ultimately yielding more credible (rich, varied, thorough) assessment evidence of Core Standards. Once in place, [this] will enable students to graduate from high school with a résumé of accomplishment compiled over their school career, rather than simply a transcript of courses taken, "seat time" logged, and a cumulative GPA. (p. 8)

A Compendium of Indicators

In view of the "photo album" approach as a rich assessment of student performance, here is how we view the roles of various test types and tasks.

External tests. External tests can measure declarative and procedural knowledge, analysis, and limited application. As these tests are snapshots in a larger photo album, they provide valid information of student achievement.

However, if test-taking inappropriately dominates daily instruction, it has a chilling effect on engagement and overall results. Grant Wiggins often used a medical analogy of taking a stress test at the doctor's office as a barometer of health. To improve results, patients don't practice the stress test; they focus on nutrition, daily exercise, and sleep to improve on those handful of minutes on the treadmill.

Revised external tests (for example, ACT and Advanced Placement tests) and newer tests on the scene (the College and Work Readiness Assessment [CWRA] and the Smarter Balanced assessments) include more questions and problems that require critical analysis, problem solving, and justification using evidence. In addition, a handful of U.S. states—such as New York, Washington, and New Hampshire—have established, or are working to establish, performance tasks to measure the degree to which students can apply content knowledge and skill to novel situations as well as measure standards that are more difficult to capture and quantify.

Local tests and performance tasks. Local tests and performance tasks can measure key disciplinary, cross-disciplinary, and dispositional goals. This includes structured- and constructed-response exams as well as simulated and real products and performances. Although many of these local tests and performance assessments currently exist, the alignment to the range of goals and dispositions may be off, which requires a fine-tuning of assessments.

Figure 4.4 shows how this "fine-tuning" would play out for the topic of "how-to" writing, inspired by the work that one of us did with Carrollton-Farmers Branch Independent School District in Texas.

Co-curricular accomplishments. Co-curricular, or "beyond-the-school-day," accomplishments provide ways to measure key disciplinary, cross-disciplinary, and dispositional goals. Many students are engaged in solving complex problems, developing ideas, and collaborating to achieve a common goal outside of school. Although these endeavors may not have been assigned and scored by a teacher, they offer valuable insight into what students are able to do with what they know. Students can describe how a completed project or challenge met target goals, archive their work, and include outside evaluators (for example an employer, a nonprofit contact person, peers on a virtual network) to describe the impact of the performance on both process and product.

Personalized tasks. Personalized tasks can measure key disciplinary, cross-disciplinary, and dispositional goals. We described such personalized tasks, where students are co-creators or drivers, earlier in the chapter.

Portfolios and exhibitions. Portfolios and exhibitions are powerful ways for students to collect accomplishments and offer commentary on what this reveals about their range of experiences, their ability to develop ideas, and their capacity to work through problems. Portfolios and exhibitions honor the idea that the world doesn't care what you know; rather, it cares what you *do* with what you know (Wagner, 2015).

FIGURE 4.4

Performance Assessments Fine-Tuned to Goals and Dispositions

LONG-TERM GOAL

Communication: Convey information, ideas, or emotions using a variety of media to targeted audiences for a given purpose.

RELATED WRITING STANDARD

CCSS.ELA-LITERACY.CCRA.W.4

Key Standard: Produce clear and coherent writing in which the development, organization, and style are appropriate to task, purpose, and audience.

RELATED COMPETENCIES AND HABITS OF MIND

- Clearly describe each step through words, illustrations, or images. *Thinking and communicating with clarity and precision*

- Organize steps based on testing and revising. *Striving for accuracy*

- Add necessary details based on knowledge of target audience. *Listening with understanding and empathy*

SAMPLE PERFORMANCE ASSESSMENTS

Lower Elementary: The dentist wants to create a list of instructions to make sure kids brush their teeth well. She asked you to do it for her because you are good at knowing how kids talk and how they brush their teeth. You can prepare to write your instructions by role-playing, storyboarding, pair-share, or brainstorming. Make sure you test out what you write by going home and thinking about it when you are brushing your teeth and revising your example.

Upper Elementary: Select a musical instrument that you like. (*Note:* For students with no musical instrument experience, bring instruments into the classroom, such as bells, maracas, tambourines, drums, or recorders *or* have the music teacher work on this lesson during the activity period). Produce a description for someone who has never touched the instrument, explaining what they need to do to produce sound. (*Note:* A more sophisticated version would be to describe how to get a range of sounds or improve the quality of sound—for example, different rhythms on a drum, chords on a piano that harmonize, or a note on a recorder without the squeak.)

Middle/High School: Think of something you are expert at (e.g., playing the piano, doing a wheelie on a skateboard, using a social media platform). Create a tutorial on how to do it using writing, illustrations, and images. To hone your instructions, test your tutorial out on someone who is new to this skill or who attempted it before but got frustrated and stopped. Pay attention to how they feel as well as their performance to make the language, description, and tone clearer and more compassionate for your target audience.

One powerful example comes from a combined middle/high school in Vermont, where students develop portfolios and create a formal exhibition to document learning through diverse learning experiences (e.g., online courses, apprenticeships, vocational programs, internships). Students gather evidence around essential competencies and design an hourlong presentation to peers, advisors, mentors, and parents. (For more information about the school and its personalized learning program, see Clarke, 2013.)

A second model comes from High Tech High School in San Diego, where students are expected to create and update a digital portfolio of their accomplishments that provides a comprehensive look at their work and documents learning over time. Exhibitions also are required at a range of schools such as Changemaker High School in Arizona and Animus High School in Colorado.

At the Greenwich High School (GHS) Innovation Lab in Connecticut, they use exhibitions to feature student work and help gauge student progress and learning. GHS Innovation Lab STEM teacher Brian Walach describes how liberating—and perhaps unnerving—it is for students to share their work with someone beyond the teacher. He tells his students, "I'm excited about your ideas. Now, go make someone *else* excited about them." GHS Innovation Lab STEM teacher Sarah Golden adds two more key benefits of exhibitions: They create a level of urgency that helps students focus on timelines, and they encourage students to consult with experts in the field whenever they get stuck.

The advantages: A portfolio or exhibition is a collection of student artifacts that showcase the development of ideas and the achievement of desired results (competencies). When we examine it through the four filters of personalized learning, its benefits are clear:

 Voice: Students can play a much more prominent role in assessing their own work. They can share this information at teacher-parent-student conferences, where they can use the collection of artifacts to celebrate strengths and identify challenges they face.

 Co-creation: By elevating students to partners in evaluation, they become a significant part of the goal-setting process, and they help decide on next steps to take in subsequent projects or performances.

Social construction: Students see that they can continue to improve by candidly looking at their current work and developing an actionable set of next steps in consultation with the teacher, advisor, or employer, whatever the case may be.

 Self-discovery: Students uncover areas of growth and achievement that often get lost in a traditional grading structure. They also learn to describe themselves as learners in richer ways than as simply "good" or "bad" at something.

The cautions: The implementation of portfolios and exhibitions can be cumbersome—a drain on the energy and resources of both teacher and student. *Students* may struggle to see the value of the collection and may engage in superficial reflections. *Teachers* may struggle to figure out how to incorporate portfolios as part of regular classroom practice and how to evaluate this behemoth collection. They may become disillusioned with lack of substantive commentary from their students, which makes it difficult to articulate growth and next steps. *Parents* may struggle to determine how their child did in relation to the learning goals or competencies and what specific guidance they need to give to support their child's next steps. In the absence of tight alignment between the collection and the goals and competencies, parents are relegated to the role of audience member for the work.

Recommendations for Making Portfolios and Exhibitions Work

Consistency is key. Collecting student artifacts is only a small part of the larger point, which is demonstrating growth over long periods of time. The cycle of collection, reflection, and action must be meaningfully integrated into the learning process for both teacher and student. For example, kindergarten students might collect their work over the course of a week in pizza boxes (easy to stack!). Each Friday, the students went through the work they collected and culled those examples they were proud of, based on internal and external criteria.

Celebrate the small wins on the road to achievement. These types of celebrations are not driven by grades, but by a series of unsung victories along the way. Quotes from talented pioneers such as these can help clarify for you and your students that achievement is grounded in persistence and grows through revision and adjustment:

• "Genius is 1 percent inspiration and 99 percent perspiration. As a result, genius is often a talented person who has simply done all of his homework." —*Thomas Edison*

• "I've missed over 9,000 shots in my career. I've lost almost 300 games. Twenty-six times I've been trusted to take the game-winning shot . . . and missed. I've failed over and over and over again in my life. And that is why I succeed." —*Michael Jordan*

• "You are what you repeatedly do. Excellence is not an event— it is a habit." —*Aristotle*

• "The most exciting phrase to hear in science, the one that heralds new discoveries, is not 'Eureka!' (I've found it!), but '*That's funny . . .*'" —*Isaac Asimov*

• "It's kind of fun to do the impossible." —*Walt Disney*

Avoid the autopsy mindset. Typically, there are reflection moments in conferences, exhibitions, and presentations in which students are expected to communicate what they learned about themselves along the way. We witnessed one such example, in which students made comments such as "I learned that I'm a terrible procrastinator" and "I had a hard time finding people who were interested in helping me on my project." Instead of identifying a verdict about oneself that becomes a life sentence, students should experience self-discovery as an ongoing journey in which one changes and grows. Learning how to use time or network effectively is a skill we can teach—and students can learn.

To Sum Up

Showing what you know is not limited to a multiple-choice test. In fact, getting the right answer on such a test may show that students know a given fact, but it doesn't help describe what they do when they deepen their understanding by synthesizing, analyzing, and creating. When students have the opportunity to develop an inquiry-based project and allow themselves to wonder about new ideas, we educators have a very different kind of assessment. Student performances show how their minds work and how they behave when we're not telling them exactly what to do. Those sorts of performances describe what is called for as our students prepare for college and their careers.

What Personalized Learning Looks Like, Feels Like, and Sounds Like

The Instructional Plan

Because we know many educators are curious about the day-to-day reality of personalized learning, we asked a group of educators in Charlotte-Mecklenburg Public Schools in North Carolina who have been personalizing learning for one year or more to provide a window into their classrooms. Here's a sample of what they had to say:

• "Personalized learning looks like smiles on the faces of both the teachers and students because their interests and passions are leading their learning. It sounds like *lots* of questions, academic noise (as students collaborate), interviews, and presentations." — *Elementary school principal*

• "It looks a bit chaotic from the outside. Everyone is working on something different. There might be quite a bit of noise and movement at times. But students are working on something relevant and hopefully talking about what they're learning." —*High school teacher*

• "In personalized learning, various activities are occurring simultaneously, with students working at their own pace, completing assignments based on personal needs, and engaging in small-group instruction when needed. It can include student-led discussions, cooperative learning, targeted reading groups, leadership seminars, projects, and direct instruction." —*7th grade teacher*

- "To me, personalized learning looks student-centered. I give students more control and power. I become the facilitator of learning as opposed to just the teacher up front. It gives students the freedom to take chances and show mastery in different ways. It also gives them the opportunity to spend more or less time on a particular topic. To me, it simply feels right." —*Kindergarten teacher*

- "Personalized learning looks, sounds, and feels alive and fluid. The movement and chatter are meaningful and productive. There's certainly more talking, but it's always directed toward collaboration, support, and learning. No longer is the room arranged for one teaching or learning style; the room has become flexible, and students move throughout it as needed to support how they learn best. The students are highly motivated and invested in their learning. The energy of the room is intensified because students are completing tasks that are challenging and leveled just for them." —*Support staff member*

- "Students are more independent and reflective of their work. They can explain the activity they're doing and how it's helping them, and they're collaborative and motivated to complete assignments and help one another. Students are engaged and enjoy working hard to achieve their goals." —*1st grade teacher*

- "Personalized learning has made me realize that good teaching doesn't take place by teaching a list of objectives, but by intentionally planning ways for students to create their own learning. Planning starts with objectives, but outcomes are not limited by them. Rather, they're directed by the students' desires and explorations." —*4th grade teacher*

In this chapter, we turn our attention to the daily reality of personalized learning—its sequence, its pace, and how students interact with content. As the Charlotte-Mecklenburg educators attest, it's a balance of things happening simultaneously. It's distinguished by a great deal of flexibility, collaboration, and creativity. When teachers commit to meeting students where they are, inviting them to the design table and listening to what fascinates them, what their struggles are, and how they want to demonstrate learning, an old-fashioned, one-size-fits-all approach to teaching and learning is no longer viable. As educator Michael Fisher (2015) has argued, "The time has come to modernize our teaching methods. Instructional nostalgia won't work anymore" (p. 2).

The Instructional Plan: The Structured Process of Personalization

Key Element	Role of the Student and the Teacher	Related Habits of Mind
INSTRUCTIONAL PLAN *What does designing a learning plan look like?*	Student and teacher collaborate to create an instructional plan for learning. They consider sequence, pace, and content, based on student interest and need. Student and teacher continuously revisit the plan to modify or innovate, based on assessment of progress.	• Questioning and problem posing • Creating, imagining, and innovating • Managing impulsivity • Thinking about your thinking • Persisting

Personalized learning doesn't come about just because a teacher decides it is worth doing or even makes a commitment to do it. There is a good deal of work required—*different* work—from the teacher and from the students. It's true that personalized learning may look "messy," even chaotic, to outsiders, but there is a carefully crafted **instructional plan** in play, characterized by structures put in place to

• Respond to each student as a whole child and reflect that student's psychosocial development.

• Convert the classroom into a self-directed, learner-centered environment.

• Set necessary boundaries while remaining open to innovation and new ideas.

• Call on each student to reflect on learning for transfer.

Let's look at how to this plan is laid out and implemented—and the Habits of Mind required to make it successful.

Responding to Students' Psychosocial Development

Research identifies four psychosocial attributes that positively affect student achievement, regardless of instructional model used (Farrington et al., 2012). We contend that in order for students to engage in the messiness of personalized learning, these attributes are more than just beneficial; they are essential.

Relevance: "This work has value for me."

The work challenges the student to apply his or her unique understanding to complex and intriguing problems. Students immerse themselves in an idea or investigation because they believe it can have an impact on themselves and others. Teachers network with experts and colleagues to design authentic problems, challenges, and ideas; use authentic criteria based on industry standards or professional expectations; and seek out authentic audiences with whom students can share their work and from whom they can receive feedback to help them improve. All of this requires *remaining open to continuous learning, questioning and problem posing*, and *drawing from past knowledge and applying it to new situations.*

Growth Mindset: "My ability and confidence grow with my effort."

The growth mindset, which Carol Dweck (2006) has written about extensively, speaks to the belief that we all can learn, that we realize we can get better. Students persist in believing they can improve, whether success comes easily or proves to be more elusive. The teacher provides candid and constructive feedback to facilitate thinking and development.

Courtney Hawes (2016), a humanities teacher in the Greenwich High School Innovation Lab, has explained her take on mindset:

> When a student shares a draft of a piece of writing or reveals a project in a state of flux, she is embracing the risks and rewards of self-improvement. When experiencing constructive criticism, the recipient often starts from a position of perceived weakness. Once in this mindset, it becomes difficult to take in new information and even more difficult to change. However, if we approach this from a mindset that constructive criticism is actually about building on one's strengths and that the recommendations are from a teacher who genuinely cares, we can reduce negative reactions like fear and aggression and encourage the integration of new learning. (para. 6)

The act of sharing work and being open to improvement requires real courage. A learner must use and develop further the habits of *taking responsible risks, remaining open to continuous learning, thinking flexibly,* and *persisting.*

Self-Efficacy: "I can succeed at this."

Self-efficacy refers to how we manage our learning: how we plan for, act on, and monitor our progress. Students use tools to manage time, manage resources, and work with others; take ownership for their learning plan and progress monitoring; and reflect on progress toward reaching goals. Teachers provide strategies and tools (organizational, time management) to encourage students to accomplish their goals and reflect on what they are learning as they progress toward those goals. Teachers also identify curation tools (e.g., Evernote, Live Binders); project management tools (e.g., Trello, Metakite's Benjamin); graphic organizer tools (e.g., Ideament, Total Recall); collaboration tools (e.g., Zoom, Skype, Google Hangout, Edmodo); and learner management tools (e.g., Schoology, BloomBoard, Epiphany). Students reflect on how the tools assist them in a given project and help them *manage impulsivity, think about their thinking, strive for accuracy,* and *think and communicate with clarity and precision.*

Sense of Belonging: "I belong in this academic community."

This attribute refers to how individuals fit in a community and how the community accepts and celebrates differences. Students find value in listening to and interacting with others. Teachers set up and ensure a safe, respectful environment that is primarily a collaborative learning partnership. Many teachers build classroom community by working with students to establish ground rules for behavior, circles based on restorative justice, and other ways that students can give feedback to one another as they learn to develop important social skills. Students and teachers *think interdependently, listen with understanding and empathy,* and *respond with wonderment and awe.*

A Focus on Self-Directed Learning

Classroom instruction rarely focuses on the importance of the skills students need to function with independence. Although we point to these skills as necessary long-term goals (see Chapter 3), we do not scaffold instruction to that end. It's interesting to observe that early childhood classes are often designed to promote independence. It's not unusual to witness a group of 5-year-olds taking a tag to hang on the board to show which learning center they will go to first, choosing a book to read from a collection of leveled books, or cleaning up the block area after they have finished. It's also not unusual to see students in upper grades waiting to be told what the next lesson will be, what books they are to read, and what assignments they must fulfill as indicated in the "do now" on the board. As the curriculum becomes more complex, learners become more dependent on being told what to do.

When moving a class to a more personalized approach, teachers must create the conditions of gradual release from a tightly scheduled organization toward a self-directed organization. Although we recognize the importance of self-direction, we typically don't focus our attention on fostering it, even as we lament when it is absent. We tend to enable students by helping them avoid the uncertainty of not knowing. Instead, we need to help awaken them to possibilities and choices, finding out what matters to them and how they can become self-directed as they pursue their interests. We need to offer them opportunities to navigate through challenges that support their growing independence.

The progressive development of knowledge about thinking and the practice of using thinking strategies and Habits of Mind can increase students' motivation for, and management of, their own learning. Students can become self-directed through

• *Self-managing:* Students control the tendency to prematurely leap to conclusions by *managing their impulsivity* and planning strategically for their use of time and resources. They are aware of *thinking about their thinking.* They anticipate the success indicators that may be used to assess their work, and they consider alternative approaches to showing what they know because they are learning to *think flexibly.*

• *Self-monitoring:* Students establish strategies for *thinking about their thinking* so that in-the-moment indicators of faulty thinking or faulty processes—such as assuming that communication within a project group is working when it is not, or not finding the time to seek feedback when it is called for—help them recognize the impact this will have on the effectiveness of their action plans.

• *Self-modifying:* Students develop the regular practice of reflecting, evaluating, and analyzing their work based on critical and constructive feedback. They *strive for accuracy,* revise their work through ongoing self-assessment, and *apply past knowledge to future tasks and challenges.*

It is important to make clear to students at the outset that self-direction is an explicit learning goal. What does self-direction look like in practice? Laura Dahm, former middle school teacher and now director at Kettle Moraine Explore School in Wisconsin, provided us with this clarification:

> If you were to walk in my classroom right now, you would see kids all over the place, on the floor, on a couch, at a table. From an outside view, you might walk in and think, "Gosh, there's no control in here. These kids are doing whatever they want. Everyone's doing something different." Whereas now, I walk in and think, "This is exactly what I'm looking for."

English teacher Nan Curtis from Pewaukee High School in Wisconsin added, "It's about letting go of the reins so that more and more, students can take the responsibility."

Now, just throwing students into a personalized learning experience and expecting them to be self-directed typically will result in a miserable experience for both teacher and students. So we need to dive a bit deeper into how to manage the transition.

A Focus on Boundaries *and* Innovation

In the 1960s, the open classroom was popular, and this approach was often interpreted as "anything goes." Teachers were uncertain how to create a classroom in which students felt free to make choices and be creative in their thinking. What finally emerged was the realization that freedom requires structure. Classrooms needed to be very well organized for students to become more independent and self-directed as learners.

This dynamic continues to challenge teachers, especially with the external accountability demands that are constantly compromising teachers' ability to create a classroom that is their "dream state." They must balance state and local requirements and remain responsive to the students in their classrooms.

Figure 5.1 illustrates the personalization journey of Jessica Craig, a 3rd grade teacher at Roxborough Intermediate School in Douglas County, Colorado. It's been a gradual, phased transition away from offering personalized learning "some of the time," as episodic events in addition to the regular focus on curriculum, and toward making it the "new normal" in her classroom. From where she is now, offering personalized learning all the time, Jessica has visualized where she ultimately wants to be—her "dream state." On page 86, you can find a bit more information the steps that have brought Jessica and her students to their current phase of personalization and the next steps she intends to take.

FIGURE 5.1
One Teacher's Personalization Journey

SHIFT IN PRACTICE MATRIX		
Phase 1: Past State	*Phase 2: Current State*	*DREAM STATE*
Personalized instruction some of the time • Some alternative/flexible seating options with assigned table spots • Student created schedule/activities during literacy time • Whole class backward planning of units • Little time dedicated to exploring personal passions • Predetermined groups based on ability • Quick whole class reflection/share time	**Personalized instruction ALL the time** • Alternative/flexible seating with no assigned spots • Student created schedules as often as possible • Personalized pathways (inquiry journals) within whole-class backward planning • Genius Hour incorporated into literacy time. Individual, meaningful reflection time • Students redesign physical environment and learning blocks	**AND...** **Reach out to community members/businesses** • Involve students in making connections with real-world experts • Students seek out and solve real-world problems **Students create a Tinker Lab**... or a space to address another area of need at our school **Integrated content, all day**... with no breaks in subject areas and groups based on student self-assessment of needs & interests

SHIFT IN PRACTICE MATRIX		
Phase 1: Past State	*Phase 2: Current State*	*DREAM STATE*
Little accountability during personalized/ independent learning times … with a focus on product (e.g., "Complete the printable or workbook page as a ticket to recess")	**Meaningful accountability system for personalized learning times** … with a focus on process (individual reflections, self-assessments)	**Student-driven accountability system & self-management** … with students tracking their own data to drive their instruction/learning opportunities
Teacher-structured, sometimes integrated content time: Whole-class minilesson → independent practice → stations	**Student-structured, more integrated content time:** Minilessons determined by pretests → independent practice OR reteach group & guided practice determined by immediate student self-assessment →personalized learning activities/schedules	**Student-structured, more integrated content time** **… AND student-led, authentic inquiry projects that makes a difference the community**
Teacher-to-parent communication Classroom weekly eNewsletter, written by teacher	**Student-to-parent communication** Kids create & maintain a blog or add to eNewsletter themselves	**Student-run social media account for the classroom** … used to highlight student work and update stakeholders on projects.
Social studies "rotation" stations	**A flipped classroom** … using Google Classroom to cover content and school time to work toward an authentic project or task	**A flipped classroom** … AND student-led, authentic inquiry projects that impact the community
No student portfolios	**Student ePortfolios**	**Student-created and maintained ePortfolios** … used to collect evidence and show growth
No community involvement in learning	**A community impact project!** Create Certified Wildlife Habitat on school grounds to address needs created by our growing community	**More community impact projects!** … including student-led outdoor learning initiative & dedicated outdoor learning spaces

Continued

FIGURE 5.1 (CONTINUED)
One Teacher's Personalization Journey

Completed Steps

- Get advice & observations from WCE, Meghan, etc.
- Plan the first few weeks with strategic roll-out of new (or altered) practices:
    - ○ No assigned seating
    - ○ Student portfolios
    - ○ Class blog (written by kids)
    - ○ Reflection journals with built in reflection time for morning & afternoon
    - ○ Personalized schedules
    - ○ Inquiry journals & flipped classroom for units of inquiry
    - ○ Teach engineering design process—invite engineer
    - ○ Design thinking challenges—including redesigning the physical environment of the classroom, and redesigning a learning block
    - ○ Students incorporate POV values into the whole-class mission statement. Post in room: "We need a flexible, personalized learning environment in which we value empathy and incorporate passion into learning."
    - ○ Improve student access to technology—write a grant!
    - ○ Class blog/website
    - ○ Student-created personalized learning plans for literacy and passion projects

Next Steps

- ○ Set up class Instagram account.
- ○ Continue student-created SMART goals.
- ○ Establish parent visit days (kids determine, plan, & run).
- ○ Use interest-based small groups.
- ○ Refine student reflection, self-assessment, & accountability practices.
- ○ Continue student-led Certified Wildlife Habitat project; involve other classes and grade levels.

Source: Jessica Craig. Used with permission.

Jessica's "current state" reveals a learning environment that is responsive to student needs but also holds students accountable for directing what they learn, how they learn, and how they demonstrate learning. As she works to balance required learning with opportunities for flexible experiences, her students act as co-creators of their curriculum. In the "completed steps" and "next steps," you can see how far her personalization journey has taken her and her students as well as the exciting terrain ahead.

Teachers need to help students plan for and function in this Dream State. Let's look at the planning template in Figure 5.2. To fill it in, a teacher not only needs to be aware of goals but also needs to be thinking about how to create enough structure in the assignment so students will know the boundaries of their freedom of choice.

FIGURE 5.2
A Teacher-Driven Planning Template

DESIRED RESULTS	ASSESSMENT EVIDENCE	LEARNING PLAN	
Goals What content, process, and dispositional goals will students focus on?	**Performances/ Products** What tasks will I share as exemplars? How will I invite student creativity? How will I clarify guidelines? How will I grade this work?	**Essential Questions** What broad questions will unify the personalized explorations? How will I model an inquiry approach?	**Learning Objectives** What short-term expectations will focus students on what they should know and be able to do as a result of their task?
Standards What standards are aligned to these goals?	**Additional Assessments** How will I evaluate students' current content understanding and skill levels? How will I provide feedback for growth?	**Playlists, Resources, Suggested Sequences** What websites, software platforms, or other resources will I provide? What material will I need to teach to the whole class? What guided workshop topics will I offer based on student choice/need?	

Students might use the template shown in Figure 5.3, which pairs task characteristics with Habits of Minds, to prepare for a project-planning conference with the teacher. Teachers can use this same template to help students think about time management, possible project partners, and the resources they might need. As students develop their projects, they should modify the plan and document the changes. (Some teachers ask students to document those changes as part of a process journal.) The act of analyzing shifts in project plans helps students realize that all project plans are an approximation. It can drive home the power of planning as well as the power of being open to realities that get in the way of the plan. Very often, students observe how they persisted through many iterations of plans and what that persistence led to.

FIGURE 5.3
A Student-Driven Planning Template

TASK CHARACTERISTICS	POSSIBLE DESIGN AND PERFORMANCE OPPORTUNITIES	HABITS OF MIND TO USE
What is my focus, idea, or driving question? Why is it important?		*Questioning and problem posing; gathering data with all five senses; thinking about thinking*
What do I think my deliverable could be? Who is my target audience?		*Creating, imagining, and innovating; thinking flexibly; taking responsible risks*
What criteria should be used to judge my work?		*Communicating with clarity and precision; striving for accuracy*
How will I go about doing the work? Who could I enlist to help me? Where will I go for information and guidance?		*Applying past knowledge, listening with understanding and empathy, taking responsible risks, thinking*

Co-Creating a Biology Project

High school biology teacher Craig Gastauer described for us an example of how he and his students work collaboratively to co-create a learning project. Notice his questioning strategy as he follows a process that resembles the one presented in Figure 5.3:

This project began with **students taking on a learning task.** In this case, they set out to learn about large molecules (carbohydrates, lipids, proteins, and nucleic acids) needed for life. Questions I provided to help students identify their focus included

- "Why study this content?"
- "What debates concerning this content have you heard of?"
- "What larger issues in the world are related to this content?"

Next, as step 2, **students brainstormed specific questions to narrow their focus** to one problem within the larger issue. Many students who initially struggled to personalize the task or challenge were able to build on the ideas of others and add these questions to the list I provided for them to consider. Here are some examples:

- As a high school student athlete, how does consuming different carbohydrates, lipids, and proteins promote or negatively affect my health and performance?
- With the existing obesity epidemic in the United States and an endless list of diet fads, the general public is confused as to what is and isn't healthy. What type of carbohydrates, lipids, and proteins should be included in the healthy diets of people from different age groups? Based on this knowledge, what would a generalized nutrition plan look like for people from different age groups?
- What farming plan should wealthier nations adopt to ensure growing crops that will provide starving populations of people around the globe with the carbohydrates, lipids, and proteins they need to be healthy?

The following questions helped students generate additional topics for possible study:

- "What problems are scientists examining within this broad issue?"
- "What do you want to learn more about within the broad issue?"
- "What aspects of this broad issue do we need to be concerned with in our community?"

- "What aspect of this larger issue do you think we could solve or have a positive effect on?"

As step 3, **students curated their resources and built background knowledge around the issues, problems, and ideas they found interesting.** Critically, they did this *before* selecting the one question they would choose to focus their efforts on, which meant they had to explore multiple perspectives on an issue before choosing one potential solution. They went on to share their links to sources with their classmates, including a concise summary of their findings, using a virtual tool. Here are some of the questions provided to guide the search and curation activities:

- "What do we already know about this problem?"
- "What background knowledge is required to truly understand this problem?"
- "What solutions have been, or are being, attempted?"
- "Have any proposed solutions helped to solve the problem?"
- "Have any proposed solutions failed?"

In step 4 of the project, **students analyzed and evaluated the curated research to develop a position and supported it with evidence.** It's important to learn to evaluate sources rather than simply take their information at face value; in this step, students worked to discern between reliable and unreliable sources. They also identified trends in perspectives and synthesized new solutions that combine ideas they were learning about. Questions that helped them analyze and evaluate their research included the following:

- "How do you know your sources provide you with reliable information?"
- "Which resources help you propose answers or solutions to your inquiry?"
- "Which resources support different or antagonistic viewpoints of your original stance?"
- "Which resources have caused you to rethink your original position?"

- "Which resources have conclusions validated by multiple lines of research?"
- "Which resources do not have cited sources to support conclusions?"

Finally, **students identified their audience and selected a presentation mode.** This involved determining the audience that most needed to hear the argument they were generating, as well as deciding on the most effective manner of communicating the message to that audience. A focus on a specified audience affects how one examines the curated resources to craft an argument, and it influences how students might make the presentation more (or less) powerful to that audience. Students should also be encouraged to reach out to various audiences to ensure authentic interaction with people with differing perspectives. Hearing supporting ideas, as well as critiques, increases the depth of understanding and helps students test their own understanding. Questions provided to help students determine the audience and present their thoughts or ideas included

- "Who needs to hear your argument? Who doesn't have the information necessary to make an informed decision and would benefit from your learning?"
- "What objections might an audience have to your argument? How could you break down their arguments to help them embrace your own?"

Strategies for Engaging Students in Developing a Project

The world is full of ambiguous, messy, complex challenges. As educators, our job is not to sanitize those challenges by breaking down a robust problem into smaller steps, identifying and defining vocabulary words that students may not know, or taking an inquiry lab and turning it into a guided set of directions. Our aim is not to direct our students' learning. Rather, we want students to struggle as they test their hypotheses; find alternatives when something does not work; and follow through with data collection, *gathering data with all their senses.*

The challenge in this stage of co-creation is for the teacher to keep a watchful and guiding eye on each student's inquiry and make sure it's about something that matters. Is it generative, and does it lead to deeper investigation? Some students know immediately what they want to do and where they want to go. Others may just look blank and say, "I don't know what to do."

In the first situation, the teacher's role is to help the student explore a range of ideas, rather than settling on the first idea as the only one or the best. In the second situation, the teacher needs to help students move past the fears of the unknown and help them consider options—not possibilities the teacher suggests, but possibilities the student wanders around to discover.

The habit of *questioning and problem posing* can be grown over time, given appropriate instructional time, modeling, and self-reflection. For example, the see/think/wonder routine encourages students to make careful observations and thoughtful interpretations. It sets the stage for inquiry, using the following questions:

- *What do you see?* This requires students to *persist* and repeatedly return to an image to see anew.
- *What do you think?* As students share their observations, thoughts, and inquiries, they listen with understanding and empathy. They *think flexibly* as they come to realize that they can change their minds and be open to the influence of others.
- *What do you wonder?* Students question and pose problems and become curious about what they would like to understand.

As educators, we can design a set of parameters for a challenge that is developmentally appropriate *and* messy, due to the nature of the issue, the ambiguity of how to proceed, and the need for more information. Regardless of how much students have dreamed of an opportunity to be left alone to explore their thinking, they will still wait to be guided out of habit. Teachers need to resist rescuing students from struggle and allow them to think and learn.

Personalization at GHS Innovation Lab

In a blog post, Dana Schlosser (2015), a STEM teacher at the Greenwich High School Innovation Lab, clarifies what personalization can look like:

> It focuses on asking the right questions—or even better—the right questions being asked. We, as teachers, can't be in the mode of "you should already know that" or even the dreaded "we can't learn that yet." We are not here to only teach the content, but to make sure the students know the content to the depth they WANT. As an Innovation Lab teacher, we do that for every student, and every student is doing something slightly different. One project with 43 variations.
>
> When the students ask me a question about something way out of my field, I have to steel myself and say, "Let's figure this out together!" It's not only about having them learn, but having them learn HOW to learn. The temptation to tell [students] how to do something is ingrained in how I approach so many parts of my job, and I confess that it slips out. But even then, a simple turn of a phrase has the student look at what they have produced and come up with their own approach to how their work can apply another way. (paras. 2–3)

Learning to Persist

As teachers move into a new role with students, they may find they need to get comfortable with *students being uncomfortable*. There may be a lot of false starts, furrowed brows, and visible agitation. Teachers need to wait to see what students can do and what their tendencies are in the face of ambiguity.

Getting students used to being in this kind of space is a significant challenge. Instead of giving advice when students are feeling lost, try using probing questions to help students clarify or articulate their approach:

- "When you said _____, what did you mean?"
- "Tell me more about your thinking...."
- "What are you assuming when you say that?"

- "Is it really either/or? Might there be different 'right answers' or ways of thinking about this?"

Note how these prompts put the focus squarely on the student—on what he or she trying to say. The teacher's role is to open up or reveal the student's own thinking through dialogue and illustrations.

Moving Thinking Forward with Visual Note Taking

In the commentary below, drafted specifically for this book, Dan Ryder, an English teacher at Mt. Blue High School in Maine, shows how he and his students use *sketchnoting* (visual note taking) to help clarify student thinking:

I plop down next to Tim, who's been staring at his laptop, an empty document on the screen. Tim mutters, "I'm stuck."

"How long have you been looking at that screen?"

"Ten minutes or something? What do I do now?"

"Close the lid. . . . Now, tell me what you're thinking about so far."

As Tim talks, I sketchnote what he's saying on an unruled 4-by-6-inch index card. The fusion of doodles and words illustrates the relationship among his ideas; it will help him to see his thoughts in image and line. I use a simple shorthand he knows, because I've taught the class to do it—light bulbs for ideas, borders and shading around key words, numbers to take inventory, stick figures and emojis to bring a human element. I add more cards as his explanations grow, building a deck of single-sided tiles that can be laid out side by side, gridded, or shuffled in any way that suits the moment.

I might prompt Tim by asking a follow-up question or pose a few different possibilities, even sketchnote one or two, but my intention remains the same: to capture Tim's point of view and thinking and reflect it back to him.

Once he finishes talking, I take a picture of all the cards; Tim does, too. Then I ask him to title the collection. I deliberately give him a 3-by-5 card—no larger—and I ask him to list every word he thinks of when he considers his project. He fills the unruled space with 20 or so terms. Regular, letter-size paper would have been too big. He wouldn't have been able to fill the space, so his thinking would have felt incomplete and he would have remained in neutral. Instead, he has a tidy collection. I tell him to start mixing and matching, to string three or four words together and try out their rhythms. His fifth iteration sticks.

"Dude. That's it. That's my title!"

"Good. Put a dot by each of those words so you remember which ones you're using."

"I'll circle them instead."

"That works."

Index cards are little miracles of 3-by-5-inch glorious, unruled opportunity. Whether they're doing doodles or sketchnotes, lists or maps within that white space and its 4-by-6-inch big sister, students may discover any number of pathways to get unstuck. I've long seen the value of the one-to-one conference to better understand what's really going on with a student who is struggling with a task or an assignment. Learning to sketchnote transformed those conversations from verbal to visual experiences, and employing empathy transformed them from lessons to learnings.

Getting Unstuck

Students need to know what to do when they get stuck, how to get out of a frustrating situation so their back wheels don't continue to spin with no forward progress. Although students may want the teacher to rescue them, this is a time when some direct instruction around persisting can be significant. For example, students in an elementary classroom could use the self-reflection chart shown in Figure 5.4 to show the extent to which they *persist*.

Students might recall an experience in which they persisted and were able to accomplish a difficult task—when they first learned to ride a bike, use a skateboard, or cook using a recipe, for example. Everyone has an experience of working diligently in order to achieve success. The key question that students need to reflect on is *how* they made that success happen.

FIGURE 5.4
A Student Self-Reflection Chart for *Persisting*

WHEN I'M STUCK				
1 Not Yet Started	2 Beginning	3 Developing	4 Proficient	5 Advanced
I give up and stop working.	I ask for help.	I try to use a strategy that worked for me before.	When the strategy I'm using doesn't work, I take a risk and try something different.	I pay attention to what works for me so I can use it another time when I'm stuck.

Some people get unstuck by walking away from the problem and allowing it to incubate while they do something else. Some use mindful exercises, such as centering and breathing. Some mark a goal on the calendar and then chunk out the targets each day to reach the goal. And some find value in talking it out in conjunction with a visual representation, such as sketchnotes, to bring their current ideas to light. But what all students need to recognize is that they have successfully faced difficult problems before and all they need to do is name some strategies that might be helpful in this situation. It's a way for them own their journey by building their confidence, capacities, and content knowledge.

Coaching with a Growth Mindset

Teachers are faced with the difficult balance of correcting, editing, and improving a student's work while, at the same time, helping the student hear this as constructive and educative criticism. If the classroom is organized around a growth mindset, students are more apt to take this feedback in stride because they will have practiced the companion Habit of Mind of *remaining open to continuous learning.*

When a teacher clarifies student thinking, there may be an urge to correct mistakes and offer direct instruction to "fix" the faulty thinking or approach. But fixing the mistake typically does not grow students' capacity to understand or perform better next time. Douglas Fisher and Nancy Frey (2012) suggest first considering the nature of the error and then determining how best to help students rectify it. A factual error (the ability to recall accurately) differs from a transfer error (the ability to apply information in a novel situation), which differs from a misconception error (the ability to generalize based on the information presented). A teacher who sits down with students to discuss and analyze errors helps those students see themselves as more than the passive recipients of feedback—and to see the process of learning as something that's navigable rather than magical, and ongoing rather than tied to a particular task. When students have the opportunity to understand the errors in their thinking or approach and take steps to correct these errors, they're better equipped for the next challenge. To facilitate this process, a teacher can offer prompts or cues to guide students through error analysis.

Part of follow-up teaching and conferencing requires understanding where students are struggling and how the teacher best can help. Do students struggle with content goals? Process goals? Dispositions? For example, a 2nd grade class is working on number sense and place value. The teacher may personalize some problems for individual students, but those problems are intended to measure the same goals—and to best coach each student, the teacher needs to know where each student stands with each of the following:

• *Content goals*: Can describe and compare numbers using place value, skip counting up to 1,000; understand the concepts of odd and even; compose and decompose numbers.

• *Process goals:* Can use concrete models and pictorial representations to explain thinking.

- *Dispositions:* Can *apply past knowledge to new situations*; *thinks and communicates with clarity and precision.*

We recommend teachers create an observational log based on student work to document students' need for follow-up support in any of these areas and to collect reflections on how that support might look.

A Focus on Learning for Transfer

So what happens when students arrive at their destination? At that time, it's important to help them reflect on what they've learned so they develop the habit of *applying past knowledge to new situations.*

While students are looking back on their learning journeys, it can be helpful to call their attention Figure 5.5's a step-by-step process for helping student acquire, strengthen, and apply the habit of metacognition, which is so crucial in learning for transfer.

Sharing this "metacognitive staircase" is a way to spark valuable reflection and interesting discussion. Is this the process they use during projects, when they are thinking strategically, evaluating their thinking, applying their thinking, and so on? Do the step descriptions accurately capture the internal conversations they have at each of the levels depicted? If they do not, consider asking students to describe in their own words how they work at a particular level.

Follow-up journal prompts might include the following:

- "What kind of thinking did you use to complete your project?"
- "What thinking process did you apply to accomplish your work?"
- "How effective do you believe your thinking process was, and why?"
- "If you were to do a project like this again someday, what would you change to make your thinking process more effective? What would you not want to change?"
- "What other kinds of projects might this thinking process help you carry out?"

FIGURE 5.5
A Process for Building Metacognition

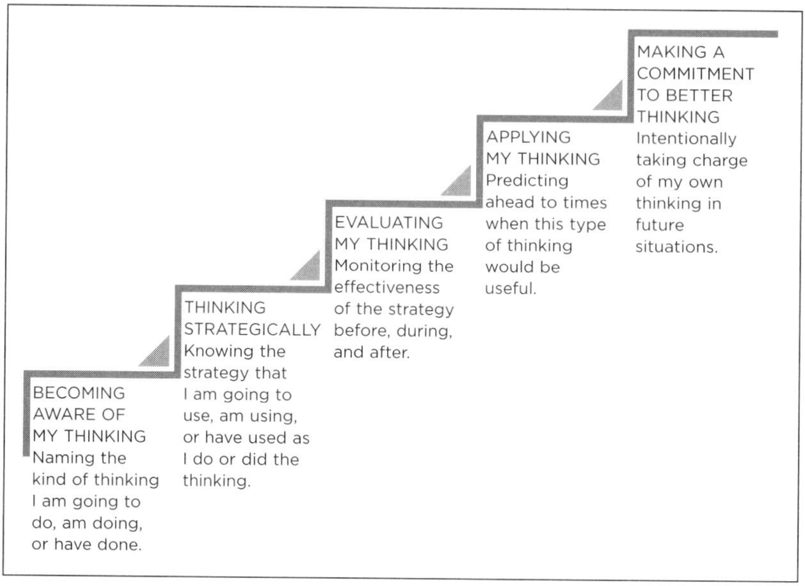

The steps from bottom to top read:

BECOMING AWARE OF MY THINKING Naming the kind of thinking I am going to do, am doing, or have done.

THINKING STRATEGICALLY Knowing the strategy that I am going to use, am using, or have used as I do or did the thinking.

EVALUATING MY THINKING Monitoring the effectiveness of the strategy before, during, and after.

APPLYING MY THINKING Predicting ahead to times when this type of thinking would be useful.

MAKING A COMMITMENT TO BETTER THINKING Intentionally taking charge of my own thinking in future situations.

Source: Copyright 2017 by the Institute for Habits of Mind. Used with permission.

Recommendations for Personalizing Instruction

Continue to emphasize the compelling reason behind the challenge. Predictable struggles come with the territory of developing something that is both challenging and worthy. Students may feel stuck when it comes to locating solid information, fine-tuning a technique, or clarifying their language. Have students continually revisit the goal of the performance. What goals and related competencies are they striving for? Where are they on the journey? Consider the metaphor of an artist who is in the midst of painting. The artist leans back from the task at hand to evaluate where she is in the process and to gain perspective—and then she leans forward to take the next step.

Be human. *Listen with understanding and empathy.* Sometimes students want to vent, to show frustration about where they are in the process. Other times, students meander around, searching for an idea. And most of the time, having someone's full attention is all they need to settle down and arrive at a conclusion or a next step. Have faith that when you listen to students well, they usually can solve their own problems. Listening well includes pausing and allowing time for more thinking, paraphrasing to indicate that you are understanding what the student is saying, and probing to clarify the student's thinking.

Remember that time matters. Meeting a deadline and task management are valued skills. Provide a variety of organizational tools "tested" by experts in the field, students, parents, or educators. Solicit feedback from students on how the selection of the tool affected the process and overall result. This is an important point of self-discovery, in which students gain insights into what works for them as learners.

To Sum Up

When you move from a traditional classroom to a more personalized learning situation, it's important to have not only a picture of what it looks like, feels like, and sounds like but also a consistent focus on educating the whole child. As education consultant Mike Anderson (2016) has suggested, "As students engage in work that is more diverse, we can't rely on glancing at the work alone to determine how students are doing—we have to pay more attention to the students" (p. 112).

That's why we took the time to tell this story in this chapter, starting with teacher observations on what personalized learning looks like, then moving to a classroom designed to pay attention to the whole child, then focusing on self-directed learning, and then highlighting the need for reflection in the learning process. In each instance, we offered examples and stories from the field.

And believe us, the field is growing. Many more examples flower every day. The sense of urgency to respond to the growing diversity of our students, coupled with the innovative technologies currently available, make personalized learning not just a possible approach, but the most probable one.

Promoting Student Growth

Feedback

Because you're reading this book, odds are you're the kind of educator who wants to prepare students to live well in the world. You want your students to understand what it takes to be a person who makes a difference. You want them to know how to approach, analyze, and solve problems. You want them to strive for excellence and live up to their extraordinary potential.

Embodied in the stamina, grace, and elegance of a ballerina—or the achievements of a writer, a shoemaker, an athlete, or any other successful professional—is the desire for craftsmanship, mastery, flawlessness, and economy of energy to produce exceptional results. Those who devote themselves to excellence pay attention to process and take time to refine their products. They review the high standards by which they abide, the models and visions they value, and the criteria they will use to confirm that their finished product matches or exceeds those criteria. As teachers, we can't guarantee that all our students will achieve this kind of excellence in the wider world, but we can introduce all students to the process that's integral to the positive struggle toward excellence—using feedback for growth. That is the focus of this chapter.

Feedback: Fostering Growth in the Personalized Learning Environment

Key Element	Role of the Student and the Teacher	Related Habits of Mind
FEEDBACK *How does feedback promote growth?*	Student seeks and uses ongoing, audience-generated feedback to create, test, and refine a product/performance. Teacher or audience member (e.g., peer, customer, family member, another staff member) provides descriptive, actionable feedback that is based on established criteria.	• Listening with understanding and empathy • Striving for accuracy • Remaining open to continuous learning • Thinking about your thinking • Thinking interdependently

We'll begin this chapter's exploration of the practice and value of feedback by anchoring our thinking in the four critical attributes that define personalized learning.

Voice: Learning how to give and receive feedback helps develop a critical eye. As students study the process or products of student work, they develop the capacity to describe and observe the work before making judgments. They learn how to develop their own voice as they become powerful critics of work held to a high standard. They ask, "How well does this represent what the author wanted to say? How does it reflect the author's perspectives or opinions?" Students learn to ask the same questions of themselves.

Co-creation: Teachers and students work together to define the criteria they will use to assess the work. They may be co-creating with a teacher, with peers, or with experts who work in the field of their study. Although a student may prefer to work alone rather than in a group, the student must learn that seeking feedback from external sources will improve process, product, and learning.

Social construction: A challenging project requires a great deal of thought. When students are doing such work, they need to play out their thinking against that of others and be open to the feedback that others might give them to maximize their communication with the audience.

Self-discovery: One of the main purposes of feedback is to provide a new lens for the student—to offer insights about the work that the student may not see. When students work intensely on a project, they typically begin to fall in love with their ideas. Effective feedback requires that they step back from what they are investing in and allow themselves to see it anew. When that happens, students often learn more about their strengths and areas to focus on for continuous growth and learning.

Feedback as Instructive Coaching

Bena's husband, an amateur violinist, decided to take violin lessons again at age 60. "Teaching has certainly changed over the years," he observed. "When I was studying as a kid, the teacher would say, *Ach! That doesn't sound good!* The teacher I have now says, *You need to work on your tone production.*"

What a difference it makes when a student knows what to work on—and when the lesson teaches the student *how* to work on it. If a student wants to become a better writer, putting a good grade and "Nice job!" at the top of the paper won't help. But comments pointing out where the writing works for the reader, where the techniques used engage the reader, and where adding examples might strengthen the writing all show the student a clearer path to becoming a better writer.

Feedback needs to be timely, stated with *clarity and precision*, constructive, goal-related, and actionable (Martin-Kniep, 2015; Wiggins, 2012). Whether it is from a peer, teacher, mentor, or recognized expert in the field, the feedback must show students where they are in their work and how to close the gap between where they are and where they need to be. Students need to build the habit of *striving for accuracy,* with the full realization that they are also striving for excellence.

In a personalized learning environment, a large part of the relationship between student and teacher is based on instructive coaching through carefully designed feedback. Social construction necessitates crafting good questions that lead the way. Students need to learn how to ask questions about their own work as they go through the process of developing a project, and teachers can be powerful models through their own use of *questioning and posing problems.* Students need just-in-time feedback so they can make adjustments regularly. Another aspect of social construction, then, is seeking out constructive critics dedicated to promoting student learning and growth who are open to listening to students' thinking and sensitive to their goals and stages of intellectual and emotional development.

Teachers and students engaged in providing this level of rigorous feedback must attend to the balance between challenge and frustration. When the struggle for learning is productive, students can *manage their impulsivity* and *persist* in doing the work. When the work is beyond students' reach, the teacher must intervene and provide instruction. Too often, what gets in the way of *creating, imagining, and innovating* is fear of failure. Students often report that they are concerned that their peers will laugh at them or that they will try to do something that is beyond their competence. As we all have experienced, an inner voice says, "Suppose this is a bad idea? Suppose this doesn't work?" It's difficult to build the confidence to think outside the box unless there is a sense of a safety net that will mitigate the possible fall. This requires new behaviors for teachers and students. Students learn how to tolerate ambiguity and uncertainty as they continue pursuing answers to problems that have no easy answers. Teachers coach students to think about the content of the problems as opposed to instructing them on how to solve the problems.

When someone with credibility provides candid and constructive feedback to facilitate the student's thinking, the student becomes more persistent in trying something new. Taking a responsible risk means taking an educated risk; it means learning how to inform risk taking by *thinking about one's thinking* before jumping into something new. When fostering *responsible risk tasking*, the classroom climate is of utmost importance. When students are fearful about their grades or scores on tests, they are less likely to take a risk. Teachers are caught in a dilemma of wanting to allow the personalized learning experience to be ungraded while at the same time confronting reporting systems that require grades. Using the competency-based system suggested in Chapter 3 (see pp. 34–35) switches the burden of proof of content knowledge to such indicators as demonstrating longer-term skills and developing dispositions for thinking.

Using Virtual Feedback

Once a teacher has established the positive growth aspects of feedback, students are prepared for receiving feedback virtually. Many tools are available that enlarge the possibilities for *social construction* and *thinking interdependently*. Here are some options that teachers are using—and that you may want to add to your list:

• *Video conferencing:* Tools like Skype and Google Hangout are personalized because they allow participants to see one another and read one another's body language and facial expressions as they communicate. They are interactive, they facilitate conversation, and they are a great way for students to connect with global resources.

• *Audio commentary:* Tools like Voxer, Voice Thread, and Kaizena allow for participants to have a conversation, although a briefer one than using the tools above. Participants might use a session to get feedback on specific benchmarks along the way. This sort of arrangement also serves to instill discipline in getting work done.

• *Written commentary:* Tools like Microsoft Word's tracking function and the Google Doc comment feature allow the person giving feedback to the student, whether it's the teacher or an expert in the field, to offer comments and suggestions. This also enables students to keep a documented record of written feedback on their work.

A great many tools are available. The key is to match the tool to the situation and need.

Learning Through Feedback Spirals

The famous quotation from Heraclitus—"No man ever steps in the same river twice"—reminds us that regardless of the quality of the feedback learners receive, once they enter a river of introspection, they will never be the same.

The spiral shown in Figure 6.1 represents feedback as an expanding and iterative process. Each time learners cycle through its steps, they gain more insight about their work and become better prepared for the next stage of learning.

In the model illustrated, there are seven steps for each round of feedback, taking learners from goal clarification all the way through revisiting these goals, with many stops along the way providing them with opportunities to connect with external sources of feedback.

1. *Clarify goals and purpose.* As students start their projects, they must define their purpose. Why have they chosen this particular topic or format to communicate their ideas? For example, a student may choose to learn more about pediatrics because she is interested in both children and medicine. Another student may choose to create a script and develop an animation because he is intrigued by what can be done in this format. Student *voice* should be the driver for a good feedback session; the teacher should listen attentively to the goals and purposes the student is targeting. This is a crucial aspect of moving from teacher-driven to student-driven work.

FIGURE 6.1
Feedback Spirals for Fostering Continuous Growth

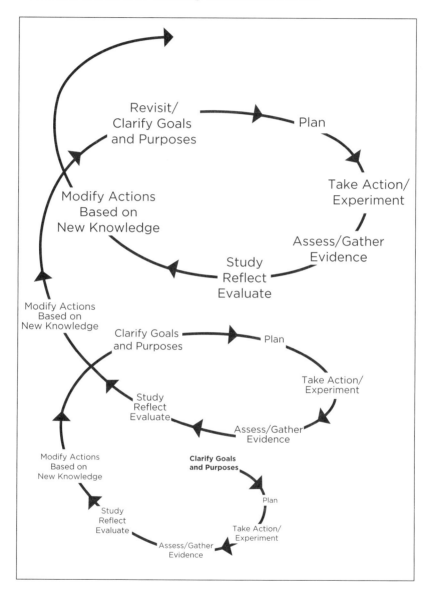

2. *Plan.* When students are planning their projects, they often request feedback. At this stage, they tend to ask about time management, setting priorities, or how to contact resources. Teachers need to refrain from giving advice until they are certain they understand the students' questions and challenges. So, for example, when the student talks about an interest in animation, the teacher should resist the urge to jump in with all sorts of references, resources, or people he knows who do animation work. It's far better to simply ask questions aimed at helping the student clarify his thinking, such as "What is it about animation that you especially respond to?" or "As you think about the use of animation, what prior experience do you have that might be helpful in your pursuit of developing a good script that lends itself to animation?" It's often helpful to partner students who struggle with the same sorts of questions so they can *co-create* strategies by *applying past knowledge* of what works to this new situation. Teachers can join these partnerships and share their own experiences.

3. *Take action and experiment.* Getting started is sometimes the scary part of any important work. We want to know the answer to such questions as "Am I on the right path?" "Do you think this will succeed in the end?" and "How am I doing?" It's important to provide feedback based on the questions the student is asking, because the target is *self-discovery*. Students ask those sorts of questions because they feel a sense of disequilibrium. According to Piaget, this is a primary opportunity for learning. Rather than rescuing students from struggling, this is a perfect time for a critical friends group in which peers offer advice. Or the teacher might encourage students to reach out to mentors or other experts beyond the school walls. As students *persist,* they become problem solvers and begin to recognize the value of *social construction* in giving deeper meaning to their work.

4. *Assess and gather evidence.* This is a good time to return to the rubrics, standards, or any other criteria that are guiding the anticipated quality of the work. The aim is for students to learn how to monitor their own work and become more self-evaluative. We want to encourage them to know how to ask for the feedback they need. We want them to enter feedback sessions with a set of questions about what is troubling them about the work at hand. In either event, formative

assessment should be based as much on the student's capacity to self-assess as it is on any external assessment.

5. *Study, reflect, evaluate.* Sometimes students really like what they have done and will discount any external perspectives to the contrary. Sometimes they won't want to do the revisions that are called for. Learning how to receive good feedback is as complex as giving good feedback. Those on the receiving end need time to absorb the constructive criticism. In our rush to meet deadlines, we often don't allow enough time for the student to reflect on the suggestions for improvement and act on those suggestions.

6. *Modify actions based on new knowledge.* When students act on feedback, powerful learning takes place. However, it takes time to revisit and revise the work. A high school English teacher we know considers receiving and acting on feedback so important that he assesses the progress students make from one revision to the next—that is, how they are using that feedback to improve.

7. *Revisit and clarify goals.* Sometimes students come to realize that their original purpose wasn't in line with the thinking of the project. In that instance, students need to restate their purpose. For example, a student who started with the goal of learning animation may find, after exploring it some, that he prefers to use the medium of picture book illustration. In other instances, students will realize that their current project raises a whole new series of questions. Any one of these might suggest the next project to embark on.

One-on-One Feedback

A one-on-one conference demonstrates great respect for the learning process. The spaces where people engage are therefore important; the room should be quiet enough that participants can hear one another speak and stay focused. And if a teacher is going to provide feedback to an individual student, the conferencing setup needs to be separated from the workspace where other students are involved.

Teachers should conference one on one with students early in the year. This paves the way for less intense feedback systems throughout the rest of the year. Also, keeping the conference learner-centered helps students respond more easily to the feed-back they will meet down the road, whether it's oral, written, or technology enabled.

The Power of a Protocol: The Johari Window

In 1955, two social scientists, Joseph Luft and Harry Ingham, developed a communication model—the Johari window—that is often used to improve understanding between individuals. We have adapted this model to be a protocol for maintaining a student-centered conference (see Figure 6.2). Using protocols like this one keeps students and teachers aware of both a facilitating structure with time constraints and the need for an open and flexible tone to the conference.

FIGURE 6.2
The Johari Window Protocol for a One-on-One Conference

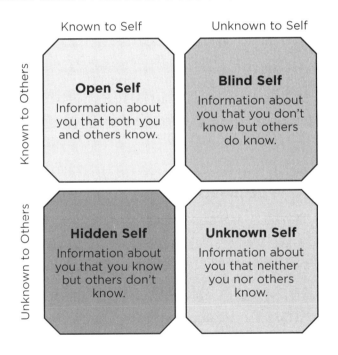

Start the conference with the window "Open Self," posing questions like these:

- "Tell me about what you see in your work. What did you observe?"
- "What do you consider the strengths of this work, and what do you think might need improvement?"
- "What are some areas you thought you might try to improve, based on your criteria for doing exemplary work?"

The point of starting like this is to hear how the student perceives the strengths and needs in the work. Remember, your first objective is to foster self-evaluation.

Next, move to the window "Blind Self." Here you might make leading comments like these:

- "I observed your work, and I agree with much of what you described. However, I wondered about _____."
- "I am curious whether you've thought of _____."
- "I noticed how well you _____ but also saw some places where you might improve the work, specifically _____."

Often, students don't recognize the power in their work. Your feedback should be descriptive, anchored in the criteria, honest, and respectful.

At this point, move to the window "Hidden Self," and share these kinds of comments:

- "I was wondering if you're having any problems or concerns you're not sharing but that are barriers to your doing this work at the next level of quality."
- "Is there anything you'd like to share with me so that I might be helpful as you move along this journey?"

This is an opportunity for students to talk about obstacles like a lack of transportation, the need for a quiet place to study, or fears about lacking competency.

To conclude the conference, move to the window "Unknown Self." This is the time to ask students reflective questions like these:

- "As a result of this conference, what insights do you have that you did not have previously?"
- "What might your next steps be? Where and how will you apply what you're learning to this situation and to new situations in the future?"

Your goal is focus students on *remaining open to continuous learning* and working toward knowledge transfer.

A quality conference like this is a way to gather data about how students perceive themselves and their work and gain a better understanding of what students intend to do to improve their work. It can also clarify problems that may be getting in the way of students doing the work. And critically, it demonstrates respect for the learning process and models this respect for students.

The Student's Role in a One-on-One Conference

When students are engaged in a one-on-one feedback conference, the spotlight sometimes makes them feel vulnerable, increasing the likelihood they will defer to authority. When the teacher sets up the environment and conditions for meaningful feedback, however, the role of the student changes. Students are now in a community in which everyone is striving for excellence and *thinking interdependently*. Unlike the more typical competitive classroom environment, students are expected to be trusted peers, each working to help the others be successful. Students have two significant roles to play: to offer feedback to others and to learn how to be receptive to feedback on their own work.

In both situations, the rules for feedback are the same. The feedback session must be learner centered. The feedback must be positive, constructive, and doable. Students seek feedback for the purpose of creating, testing, or refining their product or performance. It's a time for students to be as *open* and *questioning* as they can be. Preparation helps with this. You might remind students to do the following:

- *Prepare for the conference by using the rubric to score their work and identify strengths and areas for improvement.* They will have focused on the importance of self-evaluation before the conference;

the expectation is that they will come to the conference with a prepared mind.

• *Prepare questions concerning specific areas they would like feedback on.* In the one-on-one conference, the student owns the questions.

• *Decide how to document the session.* Using a notepad? Computer? Recording? Students may be nervous about getting feedback and may not be quite ready to take it all in. Having a record of the session helps students reflect on what's important.

Group Feedback: Attuning to One Another's Work

It's often productive to have students meet in pairs, triads, or even in groups of up to six to offer feedback to one another about their work. When setting up the climate for peer feedback, there are important conditions to take into account.

First, it is usually good to have students work with peers who are not their close friends. If possible, students working together should each have different topics; the more neutral the combination, the better the feedback. And using protocols to facilitate group conversations is helpful. (For a list of protocols, go to www.nsrfharmony .org/free-resources/protocols/a-z or see McDonald, Mohr, Dichter, & McDonald, 2013; McDonald, Zydney, Dichter, & McDonald, 2012.)

When introducing a protocol, always share ground rules for participation and call attention to any Habits of Mind that will be required, such as *listening with understanding and empathy, striving for accuracy, thinking interdependently,* and *communicating with clarity and precision.* Although protocols are important as students learn the general rules for effective feedback, they can become mechanical without modification through practice. Provide some prompts that help students understand the *why* of feedback—so that the person receiving it gets the advice he or she is looking for to construct a more successful outcome. Emphasize that a helpful protocol always begins with the person receiving feedback having the opportunity to provide the context for the work. For example, when writing a script, the context might be a feature film or a theater piece. Context matters.

The person receiving feedback will need to start by asking specifically for feedback: "Here is a place where I am having difficulty..." or "I cannot seem to get past this place in the work..." or "I was wondering what in this script works for you and what does not..." Last, model with students how to give feedback when using protocols.

The Student's Role in Giving Group Feedback

Students need to understand that they are a part of a learning community in which each member is supportive of the success of each student. Students offer feedback to help one another produce a high-quality presentation or product. They need to ask critical questions that promote their own ability to understand the other's point of view and ensure that their feedback is constructive and realistic.

Students also need clarity on the kind of feedback their classmate is looking for. One student may want feedback to see whether an initial idea is worth pursuing; another may need verification about the coherence of her approach; and a third may be concerned about the tone of his message and wants to see how viewers, listeners, or readers receive it. Understanding that different reasons necessitate different protocols helps students prepare for the roles of both presenter and critical friend.

The Power of Protocols

When students are engaged with complex problems, ambiguous situations, and idea development, protocols can facilitate the feedback process. Here are two we have adapted for that purpose: Critical Friends and Descriptive Consultancy.

Critical Friends. The purpose of this protocol is to look at work that is well on its way—perhaps in draft form. Students are requesting feedback about how well the work is communicating and whether it is moving in a positive direction. Alternatively, students can use this protocol summatively at the end of a project. We recommend that this protocol first be used by students in pairs; as they learn how to manage this process, they can work in triads.

Here is what a round of feedback looks like:

- *The presenter* presents the context of the work and shares both purpose and outcomes. (2–3 minutes)
- *The critical friend* asks clarifying questions—questions that check for understanding, not questions that offer advice. (2–3 minutes)
- *The presenter* asks for specific feedback—for example, "Do the images work? Am I clear how I explain X? Do you think I should do Y?" (2–3 minutes)
- *The critical friend* offers feedback based on the questions asked and *communicates with clarity and precision*. (5 minutes)
- *Both presenter and critical friend* pause for reflection as they process what they learned. (1–2 minutes)

Students then repeat the process, switching roles of presenter and critical friend. The two rounds of feedback should not take more than 30 minutes.

Descriptive Consultancy. The protocol is designed to help a project creator solicit advice. It's best used when students are stuck on something that perplexes them. During project time, a student might request a consultancy; the teacher would respond by organizing an impromptu group to offer help.

- *The presenter* describes the issue. He or she must briefly state the purpose of the project and the anticipated outcomes. (4 minutes)
- *Group members* ask clarifying questions. The point is to listen to understand the problem presented—not to give advice. (4 minutes)
- *The presenter* steps back from the group and just listens while the group discusses and suggests options. The presenter does not participate. The value of this is that while everyone is trying to solve the presenter's problem, the presenter is not required to say whether he or she likes or does not like the idea. The presenter is just taking in the conversation. (8–10 minutes)
- *The presenter* summarizes what he or she learned from the group's conversation. There is no need for the presenter to make a decision about what to do next. (1–2 minutes)

- *Group members* reflect on the value of this process, especially focusing on how their ability to listen and question has benefitted the presenter. (4 minutes)

Again, this process should be completed in under 30 minutes.

Reflection as Central to Feedback

Reflections help us validate, expand, and enrich our learning about the production of work. When we share these reflections, we also demonstrate our willingness to be public about our learning. Teachers often convene group sessions in which students share their reflections on their process.

In other situations, students are asked to keep a reflective journal. The journal is an opportunity to document insights, learning, questions, new ideas, and new routes to innovation. Too often, however, journals become another mundane task for students to complete rather than an opportunity for *self-discovery*. It's sometimes useful to give students models from other sources—from journals of artists, scientists, or students from previous years.

As students embark on a personalized learning design, consider prompts such as these:

- "How do you feel about the work you are starting?"
- "How do you envision your end result?"
- "What questions or problems are you posing that will focus your research?"

As the students engage with the process, they should consider such questions as these:

- "What do you already know about the topic as a place to start?"
- "What other projects have you done or what other experiences have you had that you can draw from as you become involved in this project?"
- "What are you aware of in your decision-making process?"
- "What are some of the criteria for excellence that you are holding in your head to judge the outcome of this project?"

- "How does the feedback you have been getting from your peers help you as you move forward with this project?"

After the students have completed the project, have them consider questions like these:

- "How does this product compare with how you thought it would turn out?"
- "How does this compare with previous work that you have done?"
- "When you move on to the next project, what important points will you consider?"
- "What are some patterns that you observe about yourself as a self-directed learner?"
- "What insights have you learned that you will carry forward to the next project you do?"

The point of these questions is to move the dialogue away from a dependence on external feedback, as well as to urge students to consult and strengthen an internal compass and become more self-directed.

The Student's Role in Reflection

Reflection prompts students to focus on *self-discovery*. Too often, students see reflection as just another task to fulfill, rather than as a thoughtful process in which they can investigate their inner world.

Students may be willing to share some, but not all, of their reflections on their learning. For example, a teacher might ask students to respond in writing to questions about their learning planning, process, or product. The teacher might then ask them to underline parts of their reflections they would be willing to share and discuss with someone else. In response, one student might talk about how he struggled to stay with the project when it got difficult; another might describe or how she overcame a particular hurdle. Students partner with one another and talk about the parts they underlined. Finally, they create a draft that summarizes some of their reflections to submit electronically to the teacher, who will comment within the document.

A significant part of self-discovery is to become self-observing. Students need to recognize their own accomplishments, as well as the signs of resistance—such as when they start to feel themselves justifying what they did or blaming the person giving the feedback for not understanding. They must learn how to *persist* with the work as well as to put closure to the work, even when it is not as perfect as they might like. Mario Cuomo, the governor of New York and an excellent speaker, once noted that he never actually felt he'd finished writing his speeches; when he stopped, it was only because a deadline made him stop. Knowing how to continue crafting and when to stop is often a delicate balance. Good feedback—as well as a deadline—can help students learn how to manage high-quality work.

Recommendations for Establishing Feedback in the Classroom

Make it safe. To convince students that we really are operating with growth in mind, we must make certain that feedback is always about the work and not about the person. The criteria for judgment that are established within the learning environment, especially when the criteria are co-created, can keep feedback properly focused on the work.

Champion failing forward. Make feedback an opportunity for *self-discovery*. When students are faced with a messy problem, challenge, or idea, experimentation is a natural next step and should be encouraged. When a learner is invested in the challenge and committed to seeing it through—getting to the next level of a video game, figuring out how to do a 360-degree spin on a skateboard, creating a musical phrase—that learner is committed to the task because it is both difficult and joyful.

Build the habit of remaining open to continuous learning. Establish regular times and places for giving and receiving feedback. Possibilities might include

- Mentor relationships where students have the chance to engage with people outside the classroom—an expert in the field who visits over Skype, for example, or a teacher from a different department or even a different school.

- Teacher conferences set up specifically for project feedback. It is always helpful for the student to know in advance when this conference will be prepared for the event.

- Peer-based individual or group feedback opportunities in which students work from given protocols to help them find a good balance between responding with too little critique (because of friendships) or uninvited or unfocused critique.

To Sum Up

In personalized learning, feedback plays a significant role in *self-discovery*. The hope is that students will be able to describe who they are as learners, what their strengths are, what their weaknesses are, and what they plan to do to achieve their next levels of performance. They need to use the feedback they have received as a part of the narrative of their learning as they tell the story of what influenced their decisions along the way.

Each story of learning becomes a story with lessons to learn from. When students observe repeated patterns, they need to ask some important questions: "Why is this always happening?" "Do I want this to happen?" and "If not, how can I think more flexibly and change my direction?" Feedback and reflection on both process and product are significant parts of learning, but we are often too busy teaching, managing, and grading to give them the proper attention. By spending more time conferring as a coach, critical friend, and sounding board, teachers create not only stronger relationships with students but also ongoing opportunities to clarify student expectations regarding goals, competencies, and evaluation tools.

Creating a Culture of
Personalized Learning

Although many claim to be dedicated to personalizing learning, the claim often does not match the reality. We see so many instances of educators touting the importance of "soft skills" such as the Habits of Mind, yet the profession's attention to attitudes and dispositions has too often been secondary to a desire to standardize the ways we account for learning. Too often, there is a disconnect between what is in the teacher's head, what is in the student's head, and what is in this week's, month's, or year's rhetoric of school reform.

To sustain personalized learning—and transform the rhetoric into reality—the school must commit to the cultural change of intentionally using the Habits of Mind for effective thinking, communicating, and collaborating *consistently* and *throughout the system*. These habits are pivotal to a student's success in handling the complexity of challenges, problems, and tasks within and beyond the school walls.

In this chapter, we will describe what it looks like to really commit to personalized learning—how this commitment plays out in the classroom, school, and system and how it transforms the culture as a whole.

From Toe-in-the-Water to All-In

When teachers move to personalize learning, they want to engage their learners in deeper thinking as they build the habits for success in learning and in life. Teachers need to be explicit about the behaviors they expect from students because it informs the classroom culture. James Rickabaugh (2016), director of the Institute for Personalized Learning in Wisconsin, has called this a "repositioning of the student within the learning and teaching process" (p. 5). When students more actively engage with shaping their culture, they take greater responsibility for committing to learning.

In this approach to learning, teachers also undergo a "repositioning." Perkins and Reese (2014) have suggested a range of teacher responses to change:

> We have never seen all members of such a community energetically and uniformly invest themselves in a new change initiative. There are always skeptics alongside enthusiasts, late adopters alongside early adopters. How can one foster a community with nimble legs for the innovation? There's room for degrees of participation— all-in, half-in, toe-in the-water, bystander-for-now. (p. 44)

Our informal research suggests that teachers tend to go through four phases of learning as they make the transition from a more traditional classroom to a more personalized one—as they move from "toe-in-the-water" to "all-in." In Figure 7.1 (see pp. 122–124), we list questions that teachers grapple with at each of the four phases as well as some responses to those questions from teachers at Vista Innovation and Design Academy, a public middle school in California.

Eric Chagala, principal of Vista Innovation and Design Academy, has been working alongside his teachers to personalize learning through leveraging the design thinking process and project-based learning. Although he is well aware that his school is still a work in progress, Chagala shared with us some of the significant accomplishments he is seeing in his teachers after only two years of practicing the approach:

FIGURE 7.1

Four Phases of Personalized Learning Implementation

PHASE

KEY IMPLEMENTATION QUESTIONS

- What is personalized learning?
- How much change does it require of me to just get started?
- What am I observing about my students and myself that suggests a change is needed?
- How much effort are my students putting into their learning? How much effort am I putting into their learning for them?

WHAT TEACHERS SAY

Personalized learning to me is student inquiry and investigation guided by teachers who carefully craft the learning process.

—Angela Townsend

A teacher defines and establishes clear learning objectives but provides students a variety of ways in which to achieve these. Personalized learning requires a teacher to relinquish control and expectations for linear and uniform learning.

—David Ruiz

PHASE 2

KEY IMPLEMENTATION QUESTIONS

- What is my vision for what personalized learning looks like, feels like, and sounds like in my classroom?

WHAT TEACHERS SAY

Engaged students require less prompting to complete assignments because they have buy-in to their completion. Therefore, the amount of effort the teacher invests in planning pays off exponentially in student engagement. [Unlike in the traditional structure,] this provides time to conference and address students' needs one to one.

—Sylvia Brown

One of the most important aspects of personalized learning is the degree to which students take responsibility for their own quest for knowledge. This requires a paradigm shift from the traditional teacher-controlled environment to one in which the child is allowed creative "voice and choice." Teachers need to adopt a more open mindset about each student's unique learning path, position themselves as a mentor and coach, and offer positive encouragement along students' journey to success.

—Mike Eiben

PHASE

KEY IMPLEMENTATION QUESTIONS

- How are students growing this vision with me as I make changes?
- How are students developing their voice in the classroom?
- In what ways are they co-creating with one another and with the adults?
- How are they using the expertise of others to socially construct their thinking?
- What are they discovering about themselves that helps them become successful as learners?
- How do I collect evidence of this?
- How do I communicate that evidence to parents?

WHAT TEACHERS SAY

An assignment is no longer something that is disembodied from the students' selves but rather something that expresses a part of their identity. Allowing the self a place within the learning leads to us learning more about one another. Socially constructing knowledge as a collection of distinct interpretations leads to a richer understanding of absolutely any subject.

—*David Ruiz*

I see that students feel more at ease with their learning. They have grown in their own passions and have become self-motivated to learn because it is personal to them. Probably the best way to communicate to parents is to show them what the students have done—the end product—as well as the journey the students have made. We did an exhibition night that showed student work; this helped parents see their student's success. A grade can never portray the journey of a student and their struggle to create great work. Their work should represent their learning.

—*Angela Townsend*

Previously, I was the imparter of information, and students were the receivers. Presently, I am the facilitator, and students apply and extend the content in the way that best interests them. Therefore, they co-create with the teacher to make sure the direction they have chosen is within the guidelines of the project and for better understanding.

—*Sylvia Brown*

Continued

FIGURE 7.1 (CONTINUED)

Four Phases of Personalized Learning Implementation

PHASE

KEY IMPLEMENTATION QUESTIONS

- How do I know if students are performing better or differently as a result of the change?
- How can we continue to grow and make it better?
- How do I get feedback from parents as well as from students about the changes?
- How can we use the data we are collecting to continuously inform the development of future work?
- How do I share what I am learning with my colleagues so that we think systemically as a school?
- What changes do I see in my workload since the shift?
- Do I see more students taking action as a result of their learning? Do I see more engagement?
- How can I let my students communicate these positive changes to others, rather than communicating it myself?

WHAT TEACHERS SAY

After completing the first quarter of our pilot personalized learning program, the biggest change that my colleagues and I are noticing is increased buy-in from our students. We are still a work in progress, but the majority of our students are actively engaged and taking ownership of their learning. Even many of our historically lower-performing students have begun to show enthusiasm and an increased sense of personal responsibility. One important factor in this was the public exhibition in which all students were expected to present their learning.

—*Lori Buckley*

One does not go from linear and teacher-centric learning to student-centered learning overnight. My experiences thus far have shown me that when students are more engaged and parents share the enthusiasm their students have demonstrated for the projects you assign, then you may be on the right track. And when students are confused and turn in projects that miss the mark, then it may be time to readjust and better articulate your learning objectives.

—*David Ruiz*

Teachers are no longer pulling kids through curriculum. Personalizing instruction gives students more self-efficacy, it gives them the opportunity to *want* to engage in authentic self-reflection and share their learning with a public audience. And students *care* about their learning; they finally see the value.

When teachers begin to talk in ways we have described, they are crossing the bridge to new practices that will transform the culture of the classroom.

Recommendations for Work-in-Progress Schools

It's easy to get derailed by the many demands of daily life in schools as you pedal toward transforming the bike you are riding on. Here are six suggestions for slowing down and taking notice, which are as applicable to teachers as they are to students. We pair each one with the relevant Habit of Mind.

Get off the treadmill. Sometimes we keep going without a sense of purpose. We may even increase our speed, but that doesn't mean we have accomplished anything purposeful. Get clear and define your purpose. What are you trying to accomplish? Sit down and write a journal reflection defending what you are doing and why you are doing it. Habit of Mind: *questioning and problem posing.*

Stop and smell the roses, and take a look around. Breathe deeply and find a way to settle down. Allow for silence rather than jumping in to fill awkward pauses. As poet Adrienne Rich has suggested, "The impulse to create begins ... in a tunnel of silence" (2002). Notice the questions that arise out of silence and reflection. How do you respond to those inquiries? Do you pursue them? Habit of Mind: *gathering data with all senses.*

Be curious about something. What makes you wonder? Find something that intrigues you—an idea, a problem, a challenge, a topic, a text, an issue. Think about the ideas triggered. Why is the topic compelling? How is it connected to you—to your perception of the world, to the string of information and ideas? What associations occur to you? Habit of Mind: *creating, imagining, and innovating.*

Be inspired by an idea, and go for it. Design a question, clarify a problem, pursue an idea, and then take action. You can use the graphic shown in Figure 7.2 to transform inspiration into something actionable. Habit of Mind: *thinking about your thinking.*

FIGURE 7.2
A Process for Moving from Inspiration to Action

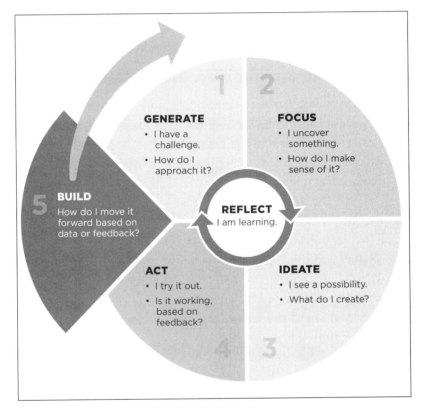

Source: From *Learning Personalized: The Evolution of the Contemporary Classroom* (p. 61), by A. Zmuda, G. Curtis, and D. Ullman, 2015, San Francisco: Jossey-Bass. Copyright 2015 by Jossey-Bass. Adapted with permission.

Contribute something to the world. Set your ideas free from the confines of the classroom. How does your work affect the possibilities for improving the work and lives of others? How does your work, once out in the world, continue to evolve through the interaction of others? How does the feedback you receive inspire future development and new ideas? Habit of Mind: *communicating with clarity and precision.*

Celebrate the journey. Oftentimes, we are too hung up on the destination. In the midst of your pursuit, you may stumble on another aspiration, a different idea that shifts your focus. The questions you ask, the skills you acquire and refine along the way, and the ways you process what you are learning are often as important as the destination you are trying to reach. What did you learn throughout this experience? How will you celebrate your journey? What will you do next? Habit of Mind: *responding with wonderment and awe.*

Honoring Community

As students, with our encouragement, move beyond the school walls to gain workplace and site-based experiences, engage with community organizations, employers, and experts on authentic project, and work both independently and collaboratively with people all over the globe, they will not always be present and together with their peers.

There may be an unintended consequence of all this variance and flexibility: a weaker connection between students and their school community. For many students, school is the most consistent and stable aspect of their lives, the one place where they can feel certain there will be a caring and thoughtful group of adults to guide, counsel, teach, and learn alongside them. Although it's exciting to think of using their work to make connections to the broader world, we must remember that they also need to identify with the place called school—they need a sense of place and community.

Even when the school is designed for students to learn at their own pace, discovering their interests and passions, they also need to work in a social environment. They need to learn how to live in a society of likenesses and differences. They need to learn to think locally as well as globally. They need to learn how to deliberate about big ideas and how to wrangle with disagreements. They are part of a neighborhood, a county, a state, a nation, and a world. The school culture should communicate and reinforce the value of all its members thinking interdependently.

School Leaders and Habits of Mind

All of the Habits of Mind are significant as the learning community explicitly agrees to think broadly, deeply, and on behalf of student learning. School leaders will be called on to practice such habits as

- *Remaining open to continuous learning,* perhaps in the form of visiting other schools, studying a common book, or participating in a Skype call with others from around the United States or across the world.
- *Thinking flexibly* as they process alternative ideas.
- *Listening with understanding and empathy* as they take into account the multiple perspectives represented within the learning community.
- *Striving for accuracy* as they determine how they will know if a new idea is working.
- *Creating, imagining, and innovating* as they move to the design table.
- *Communicating with clarity and precision* and avoiding jargon that does not hold meaning for the community.

At the same time that school leaders are mirroring the practices they would like to see all students engage in, they need to call out the habits they want to build as the new normal. Figure 7.3 shows actions leaders can take, related Habits of Mind, and some of our insights about the process.

Step 1: Think About Alternate Perspectives

In a meeting with administrators in Connecticut's Manchester Public Schools, we focused on the actions listed in Step 1 of the chart: allowing concerns to surface from multiple perspectives. We began by having small groups of people with a mix of roles list their concerns in the following form: "Do I want to see personalized learning in our classrooms? *Yes,* but . . ." This exercise became important in shifting the drive for personalizing learning from the dedicated practitioners who were "all-in" to a larger group of community members who could now express their concerns and not be marginalized by their "toe-in" approach.

FIGURE 7.3
A School Leader's Transition to Personalized Learning

ACTIONS	HABITS OF MIND	COMMENTS
Step 1. Get started by learning to think about alternate perspectives and allow concerns to surface around personalized learning.	• Listening with understanding and empathy • Questioning and problem posing • Thinking flexibly	There may be a need to call these habits out as ground rules in faculty and community meetings. It helps to design meetings in which participants use protocols to facilitate a process for listening to multiple perspectives.
Step 2. Begin to envision what the school might look like five years from now. Develop and share that vision.	• Creating, imagining, and innovating • Taking responsible risks • Finding humor	This is a time when people need to be liberated from the traditional. Using processes that encourage playfulness is important.
Step 3. Tell the ongoing story to the public and learning community.	• Communicating with clarity and precision • Striving for accuracy • Gathering data from all the senses • Remaining open to continuous learning	The vision needs to be shared and modified so all are clear about the direction. At this point, everyone becomes a storyteller of where we are going.

Source: Copyright 2017 by Bena Kallick and Allison Zmuda. Used with permission.

As a group, we viewed the responses and assigned them to one of four categories—culture, growth, time and policy, and data and research—depending on the type of concern expressed. Finally, we raised questions that would help us clarify the community's potential to commit to personalized learning. The chart shown in Figure 7.4 (see p. 130) is a snapshot of how this community is carefully listening, questioning, and problem posing.

Concerns, when openly addressed, can become strong foundations for building a culture for inquiry and effective thinking and problem solving.

FIGURE 7.4

Yes, Buts: Categorized Concerns About Personalized Learning Implementation

CULTURE

- Some staff members don't believe that student-directed learning is accessible to all students.
- Classroom climate needs to nurture risk-taking values.
- We're stuck on "this is the way we've always done it."
- We believe students need to be held accountable and learn their lessons.
- What do we know about how to change beliefs for an organization?
- Can we as a district articulate what the ideal "culture" looks like—and in actionable terms?

TIME & POLICY

- Some staff members don't think they have time to implement this approach with fidelity.
- Do teachers who are new to the profession need more time and different supports than experienced faculty do?
- Instructional minutes recommended by the district/ state seem to be in conflict with student self-directed learning.
- Legislation dictates our structures and policies.
- How do we capitalize on the time available and manage it effectively?

GROWTH

- How do we provide specific feedback to students in a way that promotes ongoing growth and student self-reflection?
- How do we support teacher/staff capacity and growth?
- Some staff have difficulty with engaging students in explicit skill areas.
- Students need to be taught language that supports purposeful discourse.
- Teachers need to develop the questioning expertise to move students to higher levels of thinking.
- Assistant principals need a growth plan to assist them in becoming instructional leaders in the building.
- How are we supporting new learning in our district with staff, students, and families?

DATA & RESEARCH

- How do we collect information to diagnose areas of growth and then use the information to change our programming?
- Students benefit from personalized instruction, as opposed to a designated time to receive explicit instruction.
- What is the research support for restorative models of discipline?

Step 2: Envision a Future State

When we embark on Step 2—envisioning what the school might look like five years from now—participants often feel restricted as they begin to come up with ideas. There are many strategies for loosening up the group. To foster real openness to new ideas, the key is to provide the same sort of maker space or innovation lab environment that you provide for students. Allow people to be playful with their ideas. Have magic markers, poster paper, opportunities to engage with resources from the Internet that encourage idea generation. (See, for example, www.mindtools.com/brainstm.html.)

Many districts are using what is referred to as *design thinking*, a process that guides participants through the following sequence:

- Empathize
- Define (participants both "empathize" and "define" when they listen to one another and raise questions and concerns)
- Ideate
- Prototype (participants play with ideas)
- Test (participants decide on some small-scale ways to test their ideas)

(For more information on the design thinking process, see http://dschool.stanford.edu/redesigningtheater/the-design -thinking-process.)

Step 3: Tell a New Story

The perspective of this book is to take seriously the aspirations of students—and instill the desire to help them discover their passions and purpose. Although this is often a part of the mission statement for schools, we rarely see it operationalized. When you enter most schools today, any story of transformation is clouded by conversations about programs, structures, use of time, resources, and accountability. We contend that, regardless of the policy, structural, or curricular change you make, it will not be sustainable or practical unless you also change the culture by partnering this work with the processes, attitudes, and dispositions necessary for learning. One necessary building block is *developing a vision of personalized learning* (Domenech, Sherman, & Brown, 2016).

Rather than focus on stories that show the inadequacies of the system, we suggest a focus on the positive ways the school community is opening itself to personalizing learning. In doing so, we cannot continue to tell the same old story and merely change the characters or tinker with the script. Transformation requires that we write the story of now and the future, and allow it to continuously unfold through our bold actions. The courageous moves that we educators will have to make—changing schedules, spaces, grouping structures, and use of personnel—will require all members of the community to live the Habits of Mind.

We can start with our purpose: Why are we writing this story, and what do we want people to know? We then think about the characters in our story—not the students from 10 years ago, but the students we see before us today. We tell the story of what we envision for them and for their future, a story of their aspirations and dreams as learners. We tell the story of how we will make learning a joyous part of their lives in which they, also, learn how to be the storytellers of their own experiences. And, finally, we end with the questions we struggle with and our celebrations of success. This is the new narrative that describes what we truly believe is in the best interest of our contemporary learners, and the four attributes of personalized learning provide its structure.

 Voice: We are listening to the perspectives of many people and, in so doing, we are noting our own advocacies and concerns. We see our own perspectives mirrored in others, and we also open a window to perspectives we never knew or understood. We allow ourselves to empathize and imagine what it might be like to see the world from another's point of view. We learn, as a culture, that diversity can be our strength.

Co-creation: We recognize that shared vision and shared understanding of implementation indeed needs to be co-created. Too often we are told, "Shared vision in our district means that the administration tells us their vision—and that we are expected to share it!" When we are co-creating, we learn how to let go of what is not in the best interest of student learning and how to continuously advocate for a personalized, learner-centered system.

 Social construction: We see the value of collaboration as we move forward in this journey. We reach out for expertise, realizing that we won't know what we don't know until we see how others interpret personalized learning. We work to define what we mean so that we share a descriptive language that helps us all remain clear and true to our goals.

 Self-discovery: Through this journey, we learn about ourselves, about those with whom we work, and about those who are different from what we imagined. We also learn about our blind spots and how we can address concerns that emerge. We learn about the strength that we gain as problem solvers. And we learn how to become both leaders and followers, regardless of our positions in the organization.

Recommendations as You Start the Work

Stop spinning your wheels and begin. There are books and articles to read, schools to visit, and conferences to attend that describe others' visions of personalized learning and how they made it work in their communities. But at some point, research and development around other people's ideas may diminish your willingness to create something unique to the talents and aspirations of your own community. Nothing short of learning by doing will help to answer the tough questions.

Use the feedback spiral model (see Figure 6.1, p. 107) as a planning tool. Start by setting some goals: What might you try that would provide new insights into your students' learning? Move your way around the spiral: What is your plan for action? Who will be included? Who should be at the table so it's a work of co-creation with key stakeholders? When and where will you get started? What data will you collect that will tell you how the approach is working? Surveys? Interviews? Performance results? How will you reflect on what you learn? Who will join you for reflection? How will you ensure that this is an opportunity for social construction? And, finally, what have you learned about yourselves and about the school and its work?

In your discussions, pay attention to *voice, co-creation, social construction,* and *self-discovery.* Also, pay attention to how you are personalizing and using the necessary dispositions to move your work forward.

Take into account the "messiness" of new ideas. It's easy to get excited about new ideas, especially when you see them already working effectively in another school or read case descriptions. We forget to consider all of the questions we'll need to answer about getting started and the sheer messiness of the process.

When researching new ideas, some "what if" questions can help:

- What if there were no school bells and students could focus on a performance or product for as long as they wanted?
- What if we were totally competency based and students could move through learning at their own pace?
- What if we abolished grades altogether?
- What if everyone had their own technology device so they could access information and ideas anywhere in the world?
- What if students could get credit for experiences regardless of time or location?
- What if we focused on project-based learning?
- What if every student had a personalized learning opportunity?

Questions like these move us out of the box, force us to think more flexibly, and generate a great deal of creativity and, of course, disequilibrium. If we can manage our impulsivity and not become flooded by our own emotional anxieties about change, we can learn and grow.

There is an inevitable interdependence among schedules, the cohorts doing collaborative work, the ways we allow for learning within and outside the school, and how we use our talents and time to be most accessible to learners. Connecticut (Connecticut State Department of Education, 2015) recently opened the door for local districts to create competencies that meet student needs and interests and can build student ownership and expand student opportunities within and beyond the school walls. State officials also quietly suggested that, once those competencies or learning outcomes are created, districts will likely need to "review and possibly revise as needed school schedule, use of time, rank in class, co-curricular participation, technology usage, grade-level placement, honor roll, and grading practices."

And now to the question that might send chills down a school leader's spine: Is the idea, as good as it seems for both students and teachers, worth this level of disruption to how we "do school"? Although a state may have good reasons to use this policy to disrupt the status quo, state administrators must also recognize that each district will have to go through a process of understanding its vision for such a change, articulating the needs of its students, and listening to key stakeholders about worries before piloting ideas on a small scale.

Don't expect things to go smoothly early on. Even when you take small steps—manage a shift in a classroom, start a pilot project in a school, delineate a dedicated space for students to create—there's a level of risk taking that is both freeing and unnerving. Taking responsible risks requires compassion and entails growth, as we learn from both predictable and unpredictable problems along the way.

When people dive into the adventure of personalized learning, they may be passionate and perhaps fumble around initially. They need to be prepared for working through ambiguous situations and handling uncertainty. When people hold back from taking risks, their fear of failure can crowd out any potential benefit that might result. They are more comfortable replicating something that exists than being challenged by the messy process of figuring it out along the way. The challenge is learning how to take responsible risks, balancing both the excitement and the sure footing, one risk at a time.

Avoid falling in love with your ideas. Often our initial thoughts and imaginings become intoxicating. We dream that if we could make this happen, then everything will fall into place. Focusing on how to make that dream happen makes it less likely you will be open to listening to feedback, paying attention to data, and modifying both vision and action.

The dispositions of *listening with understanding and empathy* and *thinking flexibly* are vital during these early stages. When we sell an idea to key stakeholders (for example, students, school board members, union representatives, the Parent Teacher Association), there should be a malleability to it so that they can become co-creators. That way, we can learn about issues we might not have seen, leverage the perspectives and talents of new people coming to the design table, and pave the way for more participation and contribution of necessary resources. When presenting ideas to others with the invitation for co-creation, the presenters should be clear about what is open and flexible, and what is required and not adaptive to changes.

Be clear about what you are committing to do. Listening does not always entail face-to-face meetings. Another way to gather perspectives is through conducting surveys or offering texts for discussions to key school stakeholders—students, staff, parents, or the broader community—about what we are committing to create in our classrooms and schools.

Let's look at two examples. First, schools can use the set of principles in Figure 7.5 (Kallick & Claxton, cited in Costa & Kallick, 2014) as the basis for face-to-face or virtual student group discussion. The approach would involve asking participants to do a close reading of each of the eight principles listed and then answer such questions as "What is its meaning to you?" and "Why does it matter?" It's an activity that helps people articulate their thoughts about personalizing learning.

FIGURE 7.5
A Declaration on Education for Life

> 1. Education should prepare all young people to deal well with the real challenges of life. It should enable them to deal with tricky situations, learn difficult things, and think clearly and ethically about what matters.
>
> 2. Schools should be models of places where students learn how to live together with civility and respect for differences and commonalities.
>
> 3. We must find the voice to speak out with a passionate understanding that schools can and must be transformed. We must not allow ourselves to remain dispirited. Rather, we must change the narrative of what education must be in the 21st century.
>
> 4. To flourish in the real world, children need more than literacy, numeracy, and knowledge. They need qualities of mind such as curiosity, determination, imagination, and self-control.
>
> 5. Children who have discovered the deep pride that comes from crafting and mastering things to the very best of their ability carry their habits of careful thinking and self-discipline into the examination hall and onto the playing fields of life.
>
> 6. We must find ways to document and account for how students develop the dispositions that will give them the courage to become thoughtful citizens.
>
> 7. We must invest in teachers' ability to know their students at a deeper level and to know what kinds of evidence of their growth will be valid and reliable. Targeted and sophisticated professional development for teachers is a vital ingredient of the development of 21st century education.
>
> 8. We must recognize the gifts of all students. Not all kids are bound for college or university, nor should they be. People whose talents and interests lie in practical and physical expertise—in making, doing, crafting, and fixing things—are not less intelligent than those whose bent is for arguing, writing, and calculating, and they are no less worthy of our respect and admiration. In fact, extended, practical problem solving and project work can develop positive dispositions toward learning more effectively than academic study. Scholarship is an honorable craft— and so is fixing engines. Even in the digital age, we need more skillful, ingenious mechanics than we do philosophers.

Source: From *Dispositions: Reframing Teaching and Learning* (p. 154) by A. Costa and B. Kallick, 2014, Thousand Oaks, CA: Corwin. Copyright 2014 by Corwin. Reprinted with permission.

The second example comes from Furr High School in Houston, Texas, where educators worked with members of the community to create a covenant for learning. Shown in Figure 7.6 (see p. 138), it focuses on the core values of care, accountability, and personalized learning, and was signed by all who attended the meeting where it was finalized. Today, this covenant is distributed to all newcomers to the school community, and it's renewed and reaffirmed annually.

FIGURE 7.6
A School Philosophy and Code of Ethics

Covenant

FURR HIGH SCHOOL
PHILOSOPHY & CODE OF ETHICS

Believing in the worth and value of our youth and the necessity of knowledge and learning for the betterment of their lives and our future, we the parents, faculty, and students of the Furr Learning Community establish the following as the core values of our community.

CONTINUITY OF CARE

Nurture and Exhibit:

Kindness • Humor • Service to others • Empathy • Loyalty
Faithfulness • Patience • Trust • Respect for self and others
Worth and dignity of the individual

ACCOUNTABILITY of COMMUNITY MEMBERS

Encourage and Demonstrate:

Responsibility • Service to others • Initiative • Participation
Persistence • Dependability • Self-discipline • Intellectual discipline
Collaboration and communication

PERSONALIZATION OF INSTRUCTION

Recognize and Value in Each of Our Community Members:

Unique roles and distinctive accomplishments • Individual needs and desires
Exceptional strengths and contributions

Source: Furr High School, Houston, TX. Used with permission.

Take a hard look at what school feels like to students. Do an audit of what school feels like on a daily basis through the lens of daily assignments and demonstrated enthusiasm around topics, ideas, and explorations, from three different points of view—that of student, staff member, and parent.

Grant Wiggins was passionate about student engagement and authentic learning, which drove him to create student surveys. You can review his middle and high school survey and read his reflections on it at https://grantwiggins.wordpress.com/2011/11/17/

the-student-voice-our-survey-part-1/. Another helpful resource is the Colorado Education Initiative's Student Perception Survey Toolkit, available at www.coloradoedinitiative.org/studentsurvey/.

The Feedback Spiral and Continuous Learning

A personalized learning culture demonstrates a commitment to change by building critique and assessment into all its processes. Participants reexamine and clarify their vision, values, purposes, and outcomes, and make certain their practices are well aligned with the characteristics of their culture.

The feedback spiral is a great tool for transforming your school culture. It's a reminder that no matter where you are and what you know, there will always be new knowledge that keeps you learning and growing. It begins with a simple direction: *clarify your goals or purpose*—otherwise known as *start with the end in mind.* Thanks to Grant Wiggins and Jay McTighe (1998, 2005) there is a design process available for you to follow:

1. **Start with your goals.** Why are you implementing personalized learning? What specific part of personalized learning are you going to focus on as you get started or continue on an already-existing journey?

2. **Plan to reach your goals.** What are you thinking about that will help you move in that direction?

3. **Take action.** What small steps might you take to test personalized learning with your students?

4. **Assess your learning.** What evidence or data did you collect, and how does it help you know more about how the approach affects student learning?

5. **Reflect on learning.** What are you learning, and how does that connect with what your stated goals are?

6. **Modify.** Based on feedback, how might you modify your goals? Your plan for implementation? Your methods for collecting evidence of learning?

Using this framework for change is much like action research. Once teachers begin to follow this framework, they can not only follow their own work more closely but also share their work with their colleagues. Gradually, the entire school becomes a learning culture in which the collective intelligence about personalizing learning grows.

To Sum Up

The signs and signals abound. Education is in a time of change and uncertainty. Our movement's time is now. As we seize the opportunity to personalize learning, now, more than ever, we need the Habits of Mind. The dispositions and skills for effective communication, critical and creative thinking, and collaboration must be practiced at every level of the school community.

We need the clear thinking that the Habits of Mind provide, but we also need clarity of vision in examining our practices. This is where the four attributes of personalized learning come in: *voice*, *co-creation*, *social construction*, and *self-discovery*. We need to use these as filters for examining our practice—know whether we include and advocate for student voice, whether we give students the opportunity to co-create their learning experiences, whether we foster social construction by encouraging students to reach out to all kinds of resources and expertise, and whether we are ensuring that self-discovery becomes a driver of a student's metacognition. We must ask ourselves: What are we doing now that we should stop doing because it does not engage and energize our students' passions? What are we already doing that we can enhance through further learning to better achieve these ends? As teachers, we would do well to heed a piece of advice from Ralph Waldo Emerson that we'd give unreservedly to all our students: *Explore, and explore. Be neither chided nor flattered out of your position of perpetual inquiry.*

Acknowledgments

One of the joys of writing this book was the opportunity to learn alongside and collaborate with so many educators around the country. We would like to thank

- Jill Krieger, Mark Reude, and Katelyn Miner from Manchester High School in Manchester, Connecticut, for their willingness to co-create with us through the development of "Student Design and Performance Opportunities" as well as offering a place where we could create, imagine, and innovate with teachers and students. We also would like to thank their superintendent, Matt Geary, who invited us to engage with building and district leadership to focus on personalized learning and Habits of Mind as well as articulate conditions where innovation can flourish.

- Assistant Superintendents Donna Rusack and Jodi Kryzanski from Avon Public Schools in Avon, Connecticut, for helping us think through ideas, examples, and misconceptions throughout the writing process. We are especially appreciative of Donna's attention to detail as she reviewed the manuscript.

- Assistant Superintendent Gail Dahling-Hench and Superintendent Tom Scarice from Madison Public Schools in Connecticut for their collaboration and support on blending capacities (e.g., problem identification, design, perseverance) with curricular content. Special thanks to Gail for her helpful feedback on an early draft of the manuscript and to Tom for collaborating on a new teacher innovation lab project to grow personalized learning.

- Charlotte-Mecklenburg Schools' Program Manager for Personalized Learning Jill Thompson, for being an incredibly helpful resource—sharing ideas and actions based on the powerful work being done in more than 40 North Carolina schools under the leadership of Dr. Valerie Trusdale. Charlotte-Mecklenburg continues to be one of the innovative districts in personalized learning, and they welcome folks to come and take a tour and learn with them.

- Headmaster Chris Winters and teachers Dr. Sarah Goldin and Brian Walach from Greenwich High School in Greenwich, Connecticut. Your generosity of spirit and collaboration is absolutely contagious—a testament to what teachers, students, administrators, and community can design and co-create together.

We also want to thank Jessica Craig, Eric Chagala and his faculty, Craig Gastauer, Dan Ryder, and Gillian Epstein for writing narratives exclusively for this book. We appreciate the window you've provided into what is happening in your classrooms and schools.

Heidi Hayes Jacobs and Jay McTighe offered ideas and critiques along the way that were immensely helpful in the development of the book, from its inception to its final stages. It is a joy to have you in our lives as colleagues and dear friends.

Art Costa is the true embodiment of the Habits of Mind. He provided guidance and insight as we crafted the integration of personalized learning and Habits of Mind.

We thank ASCD's Genny Ostertag for her close read of our first draft. The book improved enormously based on her sound advice. Katie Martin smoothed the text as she edited with an eagle eye on behalf of the readers.

Finally, we extend thanks to our families. Bena's husband, Charles Kallick, provided many dinners and support as we struggled to shape our ideas. Bena is always grateful to learn from her children and grandchildren, who represent the diversity that personalizing calls for. Allison's husband, Tom Zmuda, and her kiddos, Cuda Zmuda and Zoe Zmuda, provided patience, support, and fun writing breaks to make the experience fly by.

Appendix

The Roles and Habits of Students and Teachers Within Personalized Learning

Key Element	Role of the Student and the Teacher	Related Habits of Mind
GOALS *What are the desired results?*	Student and teacher identify how the topic aligns to goals (can be subject-specific, cross-disciplinary, or dispositional).	• Thinking about your thinking • Striving for accuracy • Thinking interdependently
INQUIRY/IDEA GENERATION *What about the topic sparks your thinking?* *What is worth pursuing?*	Student independently defines and articulates the problem, idea, design, or investigation. Teacher identifies a broader topic, established inquiry, or problem that can spark student imagination, curiosity, and deeper learning.	• Thinking flexibly • Questioning and problem posing • Creating, imagining, and innovating • Taking responsible risks • Applying past knowledge to new situations • Thinking about your thinking

Key Element	Role of the Student and the Teacher	Related Habits of Mind
TASK AND AUDIENCE *How does audience shape creation and communication?*	Student identifies and engages with an authentic audience to help create, test, or refine the task. Teacher helps to establish an appropriate audience for the task and guides the student toward a performance forum in which the work will have an impact.	• Listening with understanding and empathy • Striving for accuracy • Communicating with clarity and precision • Thinking interdependently • Thinking about your thinking • Taking responsible risks
EVALUATION *How is performance evaluated on a given task using criteria?*	Student collaboratively defines evaluative criteria or works within existing criteria to self-evaluate while developing a product/performance. Teacher collaboratively defines or reviews criteria with student(s) to facilitate ongoing evaluation of a product/performance.	• Striving for accuracy • Remaining open to continuous learning • Gathering data from all senses • Thinking about your thinking • Responding with wonderment and awe

Continued

Key Element	Role of the Student and the Teacher	Related Habits of Mind
CUMULATIVE DEMONSTRATION OF LEARNING *How do we show evidence of learning over time?*	Student shapes a representative body of work accomplished over time in a portfolio or exhibition that demonstrates disciplinary, cross-disciplinary, and dispositional competencies. Student recognizes the strengths and weaknesses of this work and sets future directions for learning. Teacher confers with student, acting as a sounding board, and helps to qualify the credibility of the evidence of learning, based on a close reading of the outcomes. Teacher recognizes specific strengths and weaknesses of the work and celebrates the success and achievements of the student.	• Applying past knowledge to new situations • Remaining open to continuous learning • Communicating with clarity and precision • Responding with wonderment and awe
INSTRUCTIONAL PLAN *What does designing a learning plan look like?*	Student and teacher collaborate to create an instructional plan for learning. They consider sequence, pace, and content, based on student interest and need. Student and teacher continuously revisit the plan to modify or innovate, based on assessment of progress.	• Questioning and problem posing • Creating, imagining, and innovating • Managing impulsivity • Thinking about your thinking • Persisting

Key Element	Role of the Student and the Teacher	Related Habits of Mind
FEEDBACK *How does feedback promote growth?*	Student seeks and uses ongoing, audience-generated feedback to create, test, and refine a product/performance. Teacher or audience member (e.g., peer, customer, family member, another staff member) provides descriptive, actionable feedback that is based on established criteria.	• Listening with understanding and empathy • Striving for accuracy • Remaining open to continuous learning • Thinking about your thinking • Thinking interdependently

References

Anderson, M. (2016). *Learning to choose, choosing to learn: The key to student motivation and achievement*. Alexandria, VA: ASCD.

Big Think. (2014, April 14). Educating for the 21st century—Global Education Forum [Video file]. Retrieved from https://www.youtube.com/watch?v=--7Dd2sAwPA

Charlotte-Mecklenburg Schools. (2014). Personalized learning: Learner profile. Retrieved from http://pl.cmslearns.org/wp-content/uploads/2014/06/PLLearnerProfile_posterFINAL.pdf

Clarke, J. (2013). *Personalized learning: Student-designed pathways to high school graduation*. Thousand Oaks, CA: Corwin.

Connecticut State Department of Education. (2015). *Mastery-based learning: Guidelines for implementation*. Retrieved from www.sde.ct.gov/sde/lib/sde/pdf/mbl/mastery_based_learning_guidelines.pdf

Costa, A. L., & Kallick, B. (2008). *Learning and leading with habits of mind*. Alexandria, VA: ASCD.

Costa, A. L., & Kallick, B. (2014). *Dispositions: Reframing teaching and learning*. Thousand Oaks, CA: Corwin.

Domenech, D., Sherman, M., & Brown, J. L. (2016). *Personalizing 21st century education: A framework for student success*. San Francisco: Jossey-Bass.

Dweck, C. (2006). *Mindset: The new psychology of success*. New York: Random House.

Farrington, C. A., Roderick, M., Allensworth, E., Nagaoka, J., Keyes, T. S., Johnson, D. W., & Beechum, N. O. (2012). *Teaching adolescents to become learners: The role of noncognitive factors in shaping school performance—A critical literature review*. Chicago: University of Chicago Consortium on Chicago School Research.

Fisher, M. (2015). *Ditch the daily lesson plan: How do I plan for meaningful student learning?* Alexandria, VA: ASCD.

Fisher, D., & Frey, N. (2012, September).Feedback for learning. *Educational Leadership, 70*(1), 42–46.

Fogarty, R. (2016). *Invite! Excite! Ignite! 13 principles for teaching, learning, and leading, K–12.* New York: Teacher College Press.

Furr High School, Houston Independent School District, Texas. Covenant for learning. Retrieved from http://www.houstonisd.org/furrhigh.

Hawes, C. (2016, March 12). On risk-taking, constructive criticism and gratitude. *GHS Innovation Lab.* Retrieved from https://ghsinnovationlab.com/2016/03/12/on-risk-taking-constructive-criticism-and-gratitude/

Heick, T. (2013, October 11). 4 phases of inquiry-based learning: A guide for teachers [Blog post]. Retrieved from *TeachThought* at http://www.teachthought.com/pedagogy/4-phases-inquiry-based-learning-guide-teachers

Kallick, B., & Alcock, M. (2013). A virtual continuum for thinking interdependently. In A. Costa & P. Wilson O'Leary (Eds.), *The power of the social brain: Teaching, learning, and thinking interdependently* (p. 51). New York: Teachers College Press.

Larmer, J., Mergendoller, J., & Boss, S. (2015). *Setting the standard for project-based learning.* Alexandria, VA: ASCD & Novato, CA: Buck Institute of Education.

Martin-Kniep, G. O. (2015, December 6). Feedback that supports learning for everyone [Blog post]. Retrieved from *Leadership 360* at http://blogs.edweek.org/edweek/leadership_360/2015/12/feedback_that_supports_learning_for_everyone.html

McDonald, J. P., Mohr, N., Dichter, A., & McDonald, E. C. (2013). *The power of protocols: An educator's guide to better practice.* New York: Teachers College Press.

McDonald, J. P., Zydney, J. M., Dichter, A., & McDonald, E. C. (2012). *Going online with protocols: New tools for teaching and learning.* New York: Teachers College Press.

McTighe, J., & Wiggins, G. (2011, January). Measuring what matters. *Hope Newsletter.* Retrieved from http://jaymctighe.com/wordpress/wp-content/uploads/2011/04/Measuring-What-Matters.pdf

Perkins, D. N., & Reese, J. D. (2014, May). When change has legs. *Educational Leadership, 71*(8), 42–47.

Perkins-Gough, D. (December 2003/January 2004). Creating a timely curriculum: A conversation with Heidi Hayes Jacobs. *Educational Leadership, 61*(4), 12–17.

Resnick, L. (1999, June 16). Making America smarter: The real goal of school reform. *Education Week, 18*(40), 38–40.

Rich, A. (2002). *Arts of the possible: Essays and conversations.* New York: W. W. Norton & Co.

Rickabaugh, J. (2016). *Tapping the power of personalized learning: A roadmap for school leaders.* Alexandria, VA: ASCD.

Schlosser, D. (2015, December 12). In the trenches [Blog post]. Retrieved from *GHS Innovation Lab* at https://ghsinnovationlab.com/2015/12/12/in-the-trenches/

Schwartz, K. (2014, August 21). Four skills to teach students in the first five days of school [Blog post]. Retrieved from *MindShift* at http://ww2.kqed.org/mindshift/2014/08/21/four-skills-to-teach-students-in-the-first-five-days-of-school-alan-november

Thornburg, D. D. (2004). Campfires in cyberspace: Primordial metaphors for 21st century learning. *International Journal of Instructional Technology and Distance Learning, 1*(10). Retrieved from http://homepages.dcc.ufmg.br/~angelo/webquests/metaforas_imagens/Campifires.pdf

Vygotsky, L. S. (1978). *Mind in society: The development of higher psychological processes.* Cambridge, MA: Harvard University Press.

Wagner, T. (2015, February). Reinventing education for the 21st century [Video file]. Retrieved July 18, 2015, from http://ed.ted.com/on/6txkqrJu

Wagner, T., & Dintersmith, T. (2015). *Most likely to succeed: Preparing our kids for the innovation era*. New York: Scribner.

Wiggins, G. (2012, September). Seven keys to effective feedback. *Education Leadership, 70*(1), 10–16.

Wiggins, G., & McTighe, J. (1998). *Understanding by design*. Alexandria, VA: ASCD.

Wiggins, G., & McTighe, J. (2005). *Understanding by design* (Expanded 2nd edition). Alexandria, VA: ASCD.

Zmuda, A., Curtis, G., & Ullman, D. (2015). *Learning personalized: The evolution of the contemporary classroom*. San Francisco: Jossey-Bass.

Index

The letter *f* following a page number denotes a figure.

About the Authors

Allison Zmuda (L) and Bena Kallick (R)

Bena Kallick, PhD, is the co-director of the Institute for Habits of Mind and program director for Eduplanet21, a company dedicated to online professional learning and curriculum development based on the Understanding by Design® framework. She is a consultant providing services to school districts, state departments of education, professional organizations, and public agencies throughout the United States and abroad.

Her written works include *Assessment in the Learning Organization* (ASCD, 1998), the Habits of Mind series (ASCD, 2000), *Strategies for Self-Directed Learning* (Corwin, 2004), *Learning and Leading with Habits of Mind* (ASCD, 2008), *Habits of Mind Across the Curriculum* (ASCD, 2009), and *Dispositions: Reframing Teaching and Learning* (Corwin, 2014), all co-authored with Arthur L. Costa, and *Using Curriculum Mapping and Assessment to Improve Student Learning* (Corwin Press, 2009), co-authored with Jeff

Colosimo. Kallick's works have been translated into Dutch, Chinese, Spanish, Italian, Hebrew, and Arabic. Her work with Art Costa led to the development of the Institute for Habits of Mind (www.instituteforhabitsofmind.com), an international organization dedicated to transforming schools into places where thinking and the Habits of Mind are taught, practiced, and valued, and become infused into the culture of the school and community.

Kallick and Costa have an online course on the EduPlanet21 platform, and Kallick has taught at Yale University School of Organization and Management, University of Massachusetts Center for Creative and Critical Thinking, and Union Graduate School. She has served on the Board of Directors of the Apple Foundation, Jobs for the Future, Weston Woods Institute, and Communities for Learning.

Kallick can be reached at kallick.bena@gmail.com, and you can follow her on Twitter at @bena_kallick.

Allison Zmuda is going on 17 years as a full-time education consultant specializing in curriculum, assessment, and instruction. She is passionate about and excited to be a part of the personalized learning movement, working on site with educators to make learning for students challenging, possible, and worthy of the attempt.

Zmuda has authored nine books, including *The Competent Classroom* (Teachers College Press, 2001), *Transforming Schools* (ASCD, 2004), and *Breaking Free from Myths About Teaching and Learning* (ASCD, 2010). Her book *Learning Personalized* (Jossey-Bass, 2015) led her to form a website for educators looking to grow in and around personalized learning (http://learningpersonalized.com). Before she made the transition to consulting full time, Zmuda was a public high school teacher. It was her students who inspired her to write her first book.

Zmuda can be reached at allison@allisonzmuda.com, and you can follow her on Twitter at @allison_zmuda.

Related ASCD Resources: Personalized Learning and Habits of Mind

At the time of publication, the following ASCD resources were available (ASCD stock numbers appear in parentheses). For up-to-date information about ASCD resources, go to www.ascd.org. You can search the complete archives of Educational Leadership at www.ascd.org/el.

ASCD Edge Group

Exchange ideas and connect with other educators interested in personalized learning and Habits of Mind at the social networking site ASCD EDge® at http://ascdedge.ascd.org.

Print Products

Bold Moves for Schools: How We Can Create Remarkable Learning Environments by Heidi Hayes Jacobs and Marie Hubley Alcock (#115013)

Developing Habits of Mind in Elementary Schools: An ASCD Action Tool by Karen Boyes and Graham Watts (#108015)

Developing Habits of Mind in Secondary Schools: An ASCD Action Tool by Karen Boyes and Graham Watts (#109108)

Habits of Mind Across the Curriculum: Practical and Creative Strategies for Teachers edited by Arthur L. Costa and Bena Kallick (#108014)

How to Teach Now: Five Keys to Personalized Learning in the Global Classroom by William Powell and Ochan Kusuma-Powell (#111011)

Real Engagement: How do I help my students become motivated, confident, and self-directed learners? (ASCD Arias) by Allison Zmuda and Robyn R. Jackson (#SF115056)

Tapping the Power of Personalized Learning: A Roadmap for School Leaders by James Rickabaugh (#116016)

Teaching Students to Drive Their Brains: Metacognitive Strategies, Activities, and Lesson Ideas by Donna Wilson and Marcus Conyers (#117002)

Teaching Students to Self-Assess: How do I help students reflect and grow as learners? (ASCD Arias) by Starr Sackstein (#SF116025)

For more information: send e-mail to member@ascd.org; call 1-800-933-2723 or 703-578-9600, press 2; send a fax to 703-575-5400; or write to Information Services, ASCD, 1703 N. Beauregard St., Alexandria, VA 22311-1714 USA.